Align with Soul

a spiritual guide to transform your life

by Phoebe Garnsworthy

ALSO BY PHOEBE GARNSWORTHY

Lost Nowhere: A Journey of Self-Discovery (Vol. 1)
Lost Now Here: The Road to Healing (Vol. 2)
Daily Rituals: Positive Affirmations to Attract Love,
Happiness, and Peace
The Spirit Guides: A Short Novella
Define Me Divine Me: a Poetic Display of Affection
and still, the Lotus Flower Blooms
Sacred Space Rituals

www.PhoebeGarnsworthy.com
Align with Soul
Copyright © 2020 by Phoebe Garnsworthy
Cover Design by Rachel Lawson, Lawstondesign.com

The contents of this book is by the personal opinion of the author and is intended for educational purposes only. This information does not substitute for any professional medical advice. Phoebe Garnsworthy does not accept any legal responsibility for any personal injury or damage arising from using the information in this book. If you decide to make a decision in regards to any form of your health, diet, or exercise, consult a health expert first.

Spiritual Guidance Workbook
Spiritual Awakening Journal
Alchemist of Energy
Manifesting Dreams
Life Purpose + Soul Contract

I journeyed to the unseen worlds for you today.

I was greeted by three angels.

They told me you were exhausted.

That you need more self love and self care.

That you aren't giving yourself enough time

to honor your soul and fulfill your needs.

They've been trying to tell you to slow down

but you keep ignoring the signs.

They asked for you to visit the spiritual world more often.

They said they'll be waiting there for you when you do.

And then they sent me love and blessed my soul,

and I said I would give this love and blessing over to you.

TABLE OF CONTENTS

From the Author

My first shift in consciousness began at nine years old when my friend from school tragically died in a freak car accident. Confronting death at such an innocent age transformed my perception of reality forever. I had never felt so alone and confused. This sparked the beginning of my soul-searching journey, entering the core seed questions of "who am I?" "why am I here?" and "what happens after we die?" to circle my mind. Little did I know that I would carry those questions with me throughout my whole life, searching for answers. My curiosity for spiritual philosophy expanded from this ripe age and only continued to grow deeper into my awareness with time.

The question "what happens after we die?' was first answered to me in a dream a year after the death of my friend. There's an old wives' tale that says if you die in your dream you die in real life. Well, this is simply not true for I have lived through it. One night before I went to sleep I asked to be shown what happens after you die. My dreams were extremely vivid as a child; I could recall them more clearly than memories sometimes. And I always had a strange feeling that when we dreamed we traveled to other realms to help others (an idea for a book I wish to embark upon one day). Because when I woke up, I believed I had done exactly that—traveled to other realms and helped other spiritual souls in need. The connection and emotions I felt were so real, my only explanation was that I was partaking in healing work while I dreamed. I experienced out-of-body lucid dreaming, sleep paralysis, amongst others, and I turned to my dreams for my first exploration of spiritual truth.

The night I died in my dream I held no fear. It wasn't a normal nightmare like I had experienced before. I was in my house by the river where a giant sea snake leapt out of the water and swallowed me whole. I surrendered to the pain as I heard the words echo in my ear saying, "This is what happens after you die." When I died in my dream I was shown the cycle of life; it was represented by an ancient symbol that spun like a wheel. It moved very slowly and when I entered through it, it showed me the transformation of energy, the layers of life moving through the ascension. I was told, "We regenerate, we rebirth, we are part of one never-ending cycle." The answer was complete. Our life continues after our death, but it is not in this reality, it is somewhere in the unseen worlds.

The next question of "who am I?" was examined in great detail throughout my teenage years. It was here I realized that who I am, is whoever I want to become. I already knew I had a soul guiding me on this life path, but my exterior, my mask to others was created by me and the version of myself I chose to display was my own power. I observed people's energy, the way they acted, learning what I liked and didn't like. I wrote in my journal and delved deep into my emotions, self-reflecting and taking advice from spiritual philosophers and leaders whose words I resonated with. The answers to "who am I?" greatly reflected the person I wanted to become, but it didn't matter what I learned around me, for the underlying truth existed on a soul level and I needed to stop looking outward and instead journey within. This shift of perception peeled the layers of truth to reveal the answers of who I really was, a divine light of energy, but still, this exploration of within was unable to provide me with the answer to my last question: "Why am I here?"

This inability to comprehend how to fit into the world haunted me throughout my adolescence, creating the feeling of inadequacy and depressive thoughts. Depression is something that has been with me my whole life. I used to battle it but now I accept it as a part of me.

For it is in my darkest times that my writing is the most beautiful. When I am depressed, the channel of my intuition is the loudest. My soul speaks through my hands onto the paper and pen, calling me from afar and feeding me love notes to inspire me to keep going. My journal is filled with positive words that flow in abundance, in a stream-of-consciousness style to encourage me to be brave and persevere. I allow myself to be an open vessel for its words to move through onto the Earthly plane, and I write as though in a trance as the energy overtakes my fingertips and expresses what is needed onto the page, as I am doing right now, unaware of where I am being taken to, or what information is being revealed. All of my books are written in this way, weaving spiritual wisdom from my ancestors and Higher Self, reminding us that we are all divinely guided. And through these writings I have found my true life purpose, my answer to "why am I here?" To share my authentic self with the world.

I have filled this book with spiritual wisdom, tools and techniques that I have gathered along my pathway, learning from various teachers around the world in different countries, and my own life experience. Some of my greatest teachers were the random strangers you bump into on your travels, those who are sharing their own mentality, and from these you learn how to adapt them to bring more meaning to your own life. I love exploring and experimenting different ways to understand the philosophy of life. Learning about the differences between each unique individual and searching for the beauty amongst the broken.

As we explore the various definitions and techniques of spiritual living, remember that this is just my experience, and it is not the only way. There are so many wonderful books on spirituality in the world, so many lightworkers, healers, and leaders. Experiment, learn, research, try things out, find what resonates with you, and disregard the rest.

Before writing *Align with Soul* I journeyed to the cosmic realm in a creative visualization journey. I had entered this space with the intention to see how I could be of service to the world with my writing.

When I arrived in the cosmic world I was greeted by my counsel of strong medicine women, a group of angelic spirits who reside in the unseen realms to assist me in my soul work on this Earth. They are a combination of beautiful ethnicities wearing long white gowns and their energy radiates from their soul with pure kindness and love. They walked me to a stone platform that floated upon a river with a grand waterfall and mountain range all around, and here, I sat at my desk to write. The angelic women all lay around me on the stone, watching in deep peace the gentle flow of water move by. The image reminded me of a mythological fairytale, ancient goddesses with draped fabric admiring the beauty of the world around them with utter bliss. As I wrote in the dreamlike vision, a long stream of gold stardust energy streamed from the crown of each of these women's heads and it poured with ease, as the waterfall did, directly into mine, as though all of their wisdom fed through my hands into writing this book. Shortly after I was shown a treasure chest with my book laying inside with the clear instructions of it to be a life manual to living a spiritual life. In this book I share many of my rituals that I live by, my spiritual philosophy and outlook on life. I have also included personal stories that enabled me to see this wisdom clearly, for it is through experience that we learn.

Even though I live between the realms of the seen and unseen, I feel the angelic energy of these enchanting spirits around me at every point of the day, even right now as I write these words to you. They are smiling with love and encouraging me to be brave.

Align with Soul is a life manual of spiritual practices for you to use at your disposal. In these pages we will explore the vibrations of the Universe and how to harness this magic for your own inner power. You will heal and fall in love with yourself and your life like you never have before. This wisdom is already within you; it's waiting for you to remember. All you need to do is open your mind, open your heart, and feel your way to the truth. You need to believe in yourself, in the power of your soul, in the divinity of your life creation. This is your life manual to remind you how.

Love Phoebe x

Introduction

Sometimes we move through our life without ever really understanding what we are doing and where we are going. We turn to everyone around us, searching for answers, asking for validation of our own existence, hoping to find a connection with someone, or something to prove that what we feel inside us is real. We indulge in fickle vibrations, short-lived thrills suggested by the masses hoping that they will make us feel alive. And so often, we find ourselves carried along with another's dream, expecting to seek refuge in their advice. Yet at the end of the day we still feel exhausted, confused, defeated, and depleted in our own energy. For we are no closer to finding the answers that will bring clarity to our day and meaning to our life. We don't realize that by doing all of these things we are pushing ourselves further away from the truth. We think that the answers are outside of us, when in actual fact, the answers are and have always been inside us.

We forget that we hold the infinite love of the Universe within our heart. We forget that we are created from the same angelic stardust that made the Earth, the Universe and its beauty. We forget that we are created from the same cosmic cloth that weaves the existence of every living creature around us, and that through this connection is where we will find freedom, peace, and safety. We forget all of this, because we are conditioned to believe that our goal in life is sole survival. We are so distracted with unconscious actions and emotions around us that we lose sight of this divine truth within us. And we are so misled from the voices of others that we forget we have the power to create our lives however we so wish to. We are too distracted from mass marketing, peer pressure, and consumerism behavior that we forget the simple truth: that we were born for a reason, that we hold great medicine within us to heal the world, that all we need to live a happy and fulfilled life is to listen to ourselves, trust ourselves, and follow the pathway we choose to create.

It's not all the time that we forget the magic of our own beating heart, for this enlightened wisdom comes through to us in glimpses. But so often we're looking the other way that we don't see it. And to allow an alteration of perception into our lives can appear difficult because we are scared of change. Yet change is the very thing that enables profound growth.

So, in this book I have created a safe space for you to remember the bountiful power within you. These pages are filled with spiritual philosophy, techniques, and rituals that you have always known but had perhaps forgotten. *Align with Soul* will remind you of the true pathway to living a nourished, nurtured, and fulfilled life.

It is my great honor to walk alongside you and guide you there.

Understand thy Soul

Immersed within the wisdom of the unseen worlds
I move through, dancing to the beat of my heart
as I sway amidst the realms of my mind.
Creating consciousness with each breath forward.
An opening of truth pierces through the light and I am pulled closer.
My third eye cannot unsee what has been shown and I am changed forever.
I am guided with your love.
I am grounded in my skin, as I move through the lands of time and blow
kisses from my being giving love to those who are ready to receive.
I honor the divine within me.
Gifting grace from my hands, let me walk alongside you
and let me feel your energy dance within my skin
as I live without fear and love without pain,
and wake up each day with my soul shining brightly
ready for whatever may come.

The Energy of Our Soul

Can you feel the energy of the Universe within you? Close your eyes and place your hand on your heart as you allow the vibrations of creation to echo through your being. This is the energy of your soul you can feel, and this energy holds the exact pulsations that move through the Universe, for you are both cut from the same cosmic cloth that created all of existence. It's for this reason that you can harness unlimited wisdom, knowledge, and love to support your life here on Earth. Once you learn how to enter this state of unconsciousness you can use this to bring your desires through into your reality, thus enabling you to discover the pathway of living a fulfilled and pleasurable life.

The entry point to this journey of self-discovery begins from within. It starts from the moment you choose to connect with the vibrations of your soul, and use this connection to listen, learn, and honor its presence. In every moment of our life we are presented with a gateway to our internal self, and it's up to us whether we decide to lean in and discover, or close our heart and turn away. When we shift our awareness from the outside world back internally to our soul, we mold into the magic of the Universe, and in this space we receive love, compassion, and understanding for our life journey. The energy of the Universe can heal you; it can provide you with the tools you need to evolve into greatness, gifting you the power to become anyone you wish to be. The question is, what is it that you want in this life and who do you want to be? And do you trust and believe that you can achieve this? Because it is possible, everything is possible, but to move to this space you need to trust, you need to have faith, and most importantly, you need to move into alignment with the energy of your soul.

To align with our soul we need to follow spiritual philosophy, tools and techniques that enable us to honor, listen, speak, and nurture our soul. When we feel the true energy of our soul, we know how to live authentically in alignment with our divine self, thus enabling our life to flow harmoniously.

Our soul "exists" in the unseen realms, meaning that it resides in the land of unconsciousness, and to make our soul conscious is not possible, nor would it ever be possible; for if we were to try and define our soul we would limit its ability of abundance. By creating a definite circumference of our soul we restrict its true capacity of unlimited potential. Therefore, all we can do is call it a name, honor its presence, trust what we feel and learn how to nurture, love, and speak to the divine light of energy that lives within us, that lives through us.

To grasp this concept, let's explore the following exercise together:

1. Get into a comfortable position, sitting or standing, with your eyes closed.

2. Bring your awareness to your breath, allowing it to move in and out without any force.

3. Find a moment within your stillness to be aware of any sensations within your body or around you. What is it that you feel?

4. Move your attention to various areas of your body. Focus on the center of your heart, and then move over to your arm, to your legs, and then to your head.

5. After you have localized specific points around your body, bring your attention back into your heart center.

6. Gently expand your awareness to the edge of your body. Feel your body. Feel the presence and the circumference of your body. How defined is this line around your body?

7. Sit with this moment of presence within you. Is there something else governing your life other than your body and mind?

Allow yourself to feel the answers; don't let logic or your brain take control. Feel the answer. There's something else with you, right? What you are feeling is the energetic frequency of your soul.

8. Continue to breathe gently (you may feel a stirring of energy, and that's fine; remember, you are always safe) and bring your awareness to the energy within your body again.

9. Allow your awareness to expand from the center of your heart and let it continue to move outward. Can you feel how far your energy expands to?

10. Is it possible to place a limit on this energy field?

It can expand as far and wide as the entire Universe! Because you are connected together as one. But your soul likes to be within your body, living this life.

11. And so, let's call all your energy back from your expansion and feel the power from within. Say: "I call all my energy back to within my heart center." Can you feel the strength of your energy within you?

12. Now, try to move your energy elsewhere in your environment around you. Can you move your energy to the ceiling? Or to the far right or left? Yes, you can, right?!

Feel the control you have over the energy from within. You can expand and retract at any time. You can allow the angelic energy of your soul to expand as far and wide as the Universe, and yet you can retract it to be vibrant and within your own body, your own energy field (which is also called your aura). It's for this exact reason that you have complete control over your life, your awareness, and your decisions. You have the power to create the life that you wish.

You can also practice this exercise while looking in a mirror, and by looking deep within your eyes. There is an old saying that your eyes are the window to your soul, and if you look long enough in the mirror at your eyes, you will start to see the exterior of your body fade, and the divine light within to take over.

This exercise to feel the energy of our soul reminds us that our soul is not just present in our body and mind (in this reality), but that it also lives and thrives in the unseen worlds, the realm of unconsciousness. Our soul exists and non-exists in these two spaces simultaneously. And this exact concept of dual "existence" we will refer to throughout this book as follows:

Our **Spiritual Self**—which is our soul in reality, in consciousness, in the seen worlds (your soul living in harmony with your body and mind).

Our **Higher Self**—which is our soul in the realm of unconsciousness, in the unseen worlds (connecting to the abundance of the Universe).

Your Higher Self is you in the purest energetic form, living in full brilliance amidst the Universal Cosmos. When your soul resides on the Earthly plane, it lives through your body, so think of your Higher Self as the "body" that your soul lives through in the ethereal existence. Your soul is always connected to both your body in reality (your Spiritual Self) and your body in the unseen realms (your Higher Self), but the experience between these two places differs greatly. Your Higher Self holds infinite love and wisdom and in this sacred space you are continuously connected to the Universal Energy of Creation, which we also call Source Energy. But when the soul travels from your Higher Self through the Earthly plane and into your body (to become you as your Spiritual Self), you forget this sacred connection. All the magic and wisdom that you once held and could access at any time is completely forgotten, and often it is only through rare glimpses in your life that you are reminded of this unity between you and the infinite love of the Universe. But the truth is that this connection wants to be discovered and we are constantly faced with opportunities to alter our perception and lean into this understanding. By learning spiritual tools and techniques we are able to strengthen this connection. And the more confident we become to receive this support, the easier our life becomes for we are able to see that our journey is evolving for our benefit; it just takes patience and trust to see it for what it is.

But how do we identify which challenges are the opportunities for transformation? Every challenge holds an invitation to uncover a deeper layer of truth within us. And as we peel through these layers of truth, our perception of who we are and what our role is in this world changes. Sometimes slightly, sometimes dramatically. But it changes, and brings us closer to personal transformation which is the chief component of living a fulfilled life.

Think of your life as a spiral that continuously evolves and turns. This spiral is a stairway through the inner worlds (the unseen worlds), bringing us home to our Higher Self, our true angelic self. The more we lean into love, compassion, and openness, the larger steps we will take. But if we turn away and allow ourselves to wallow in fear, grief, and shame, we will stand still and never move closer to our true enlightened state. Therefore, it's important that we learn how to work with the problem, how to lean into the difficulty with curiosity as to how we can change our outlook, so that we can allow the spiral to spin deeper, thus enabling the challenge to subside. If you can remember to do this, you will always walk down the passageway for personal growth and spiritual enlightenment.

But remembering to do this takes practice, as does learning the spiritual tools and techniques that work for you. You aren't going to resonate with every suggested technique out there, and why should you? Everyone is uniquely different. But if you don't try, you will never know, and the only person who will suffer will be yourself. Experimentation is important, for you need to learn how to change, so try out different variations, and adapt them to suit your lifestyle.

When we align with our Higher Self, in the pure energy of unconsciousness, we are able to steer our fate and create the life we have always wanted. The reason for this is because in this state we are closer to the energy of the Universe and in this space we can manifest thoughts, feelings, situations, and circumstances, bringing them from the unconsciousness into our consciousness, thus influencing our life as we wish.

To connect with your Higher Self is not difficult, but maintaining that connection to seek wisdom and guidance requires dedication. Like anything you wish to achieve in life, you need to learn what routine works best for you, and constantly practice that ritual, finding new ways to keep it fresh and new, because you are always evolving and what worked for you several years ago may not keep providing you with the best results.

You are participating in soul-strengthening exercises every day without even realizing it! Once you begin to recognize these opportunities you will organically implement a spiritual outlook upon view, and from here, your connection with your Higher Self will be strengthened.

When your connection with your Higher Self is strong you are able to enter the unconscious realm within seconds, you are able to nurture your soul's energy here on Earth, therefore enabling a peaceful life experience in return. You are able to seek wisdom and support from your Higher Self, for your soul in the unseen realms holds the knowledge of your Soul Contract which outlines the reasons and purpose for your life here on Earth. In the space of unconsciousness lies the answer to every question you could ever ask. In order for you to heed this knowledge, all you need to do is ask your Higher Self through the communication channel between it and your Spiritual Self, which we call your intuition.

I'd like to reiterate this important explanation, as I will be referring to our Spiritual Self and Higher Self continuously throughout this book.

Spiritual Self—is our soul living in the now, in our reality, experiencing this life, living consciously. Experiencing different vibrational frequencies on Earth through our five senses: touch, taste, sight, sound, and smell.

Higher Self—is our soul vibrating in the unseen realms; it is the highest vibrational frequency, always. We "live" in this space through our sixth sense of our intuition: knowing and feeling.

It's difficult to completely comprehend the realm of unconsciousness, for, like our soul, if we were to define it, it would then become consciousness, hence eliminating the profound beauty of this non-existence. Therefore, when attempting to understand this concept, use your own energy frequency to feel the depth of this truth as opposed to your logical mind.

Try this with the following exercise:

1. Close your eyes and feel the energetic exterior of your body.

2. Next, expand your awareness past your body and to the exterior of your house or apartment.

3. From here, try to feel the boundaries of your city, and then your country.

4. Then move your awareness to the circumference of the Earth.

5. Bring your awareness past the Earth and now to the Universe; try to keep moving your awareness to expand across the Universe and attempt to define this space, to create a barrier to signal that it is the end.

Are you having difficulty? Can you feel that pull to continue moving? A desire to keep spreading your energy wider and wider? It's not possible to define the Universe, because the Universe is undefinable. The Universe consists of vibrating energy that is constantly expanding in abundance. This is the energy of the unseen worlds. If we were to define this space, it would not reflect the true expression of that which is the Universe—a space that holds no limits and no boundaries.

The unseen worlds are also referred to as a cosmic fabric of energy: the reason why is because we can take energy from the unseen worlds to mold and shape the fabric into something material, something tangible, and then bring it forth into our reality. This is the concept for what manifestations and law of attraction are based upon. The fact that we can pull and harness particular energies from the unseen and bring it through into our reality.

Our reality is nothing more than vibrating energy and depending on our own perception of what that reality is, is what we choose to see. Our perception of the world is greatly influenced by our present and past experiences as well as experiences of others around us and also the knowledge and wisdom that we have acquired from past lives.

Just like our soul's energy, the fabric of cosmic energy that created the Universe is infinite; it has no limits, it is able to transform and evolve into anything we wish for it to. We are the same piece of Universal cloth, both the creator and the created.

But the things we create in reality (bring into our consciousness) aren't just limited to physical objects; we can create our thoughts and feelings too. And with this creation comes our perception of reality, our unique lens we use to view the world, which can be changed as we desire.

This is how the spiritual expression "you are God" was formulated. Because our soul is created from the infinite energy of the Universe, we can harness this Universal Energy and create our reality however we wish. Because we are viewing our reality based on what unconscious energy we choose to bring into our consciousness. And the energy that we choose to bring into our consciousness is viewed through our perception of the world. This perception is greatly influenced from our own belief system which is created from our life experiences, past life experiences, and the experiences of our ancestors.

The energy of the Universe that we feel can be referred to as "Universal Love" in spirituality, or "God" in many religions. In addition to the Universal Energy/ God, we can also feel different energies around us, such as the presence of our ancestors, loved ones who have passed, curious spirits, and angelic beings. We know they exist because we can feel the difference in their energy versus the energy of the Universe, or our own energies. Or perhaps you have had supernatural occurrences play out around you, proving to you that these exterior energies in the unseen worlds exist.

Religions are a tool of divination that enables people on Earth to connect with the cosmic, unseen worlds. Religious texts, hymns of prayer and devotion are all spiritual practices that alter our current vibration closer to the cosmic space. And this is why spirituality and religion are so closely entwined, because they heavily focus on the same purpose—to change the energetic frequency of your soul to invite in peace, love, unity, and clarity.

Although spirituality refers to the belief that God is within, compared to the many religious beliefs that God is an outside force, religion still admires the connectedness between all living creatures, their respect for each other, and praises the beauty of the world in the same way. Aside from God being an outside force, (although some modern religions have now adapted to state that God is both within and

Page 25

above), the other main difference is that religion provides guidance of life through a set of rules and regulations in accordance to what is right and wrong. Whereas through spirituality, we observe our actions and develop empathic qualities to inspire self-awareness and reveal an ethical interpretation of right and wrong through our own feelings and experiences. Spirituality relies on ourselves to create the world around us to be beautiful and happy. Whereas religion formulates guidelines and rules that promise such results.

Spiritual rituals and practices can be found in every religion around the world. Although the intention and processes differ, the goal is still the same: to move your vibration to a different frequency in order to achieve an enlightened state of consciousness.

In religion we sing prayers as hymns, and in spirituality we create the same movements through song and breath. Both practices are using sound vibrations to heal and transform, allowing trapped energy within us to be released and renewed. When we alter our vibrational frequency we shift negative energy and welcome in positive light. It's for this reason that those who use religious practices feel so good when participating in them, because they are healing themselves through sound vibrations and in this space they can shed their skin of consciousness and move closer to their Higher Self.

Across all religious studies the idealism of God is interchangeable, but the common ground is that there is a creator, a higher power. And depending on your own beliefs, (and no belief is more superior than the other), your idea of God is who it is that you decide it to be. From a quantum physics perspective, because we are viewing our world as the observer, we essentially are God. As our soul enters our body and comes forth into consciousness, we create perceptions of our reality as we choose to. If at the core of every living thing is an atom of vibrating energy, only we can determine what and how that energy is formulated, thus creating imagery and projecting the world around us. But the moment we move through this space and commence our conception of labeling and identifying the world around us is the moment we choose to perceive our reality in a specific way.

The origin of religion traces back to the earliest civilization where they believed that God existed within every living element in the world. They would honor and praise these Gods and Goddesses to support a pleasurable and fulfilling life and afterlife. This idea of early religious beliefs aligns with our own spiritual understanding of creation, for even though we do not label each individual God for their gifts, we do honor and praise the energy that each spirit provides, similarly suggesting that God exists within. And regardless of whether you believe in one God or multiple Gods, the end result is the same—we are calling out to energy from the unconscious realm to come forth into our consciousness.

If we are all aiming for the same result of altered consciousness, why do we not all agree that there is one path? Why does monotheism or polytheism exist? This requires a deep exploration of religious texts to learn how religion came about. From the earliest Indigenous tribes we learn the sacred connection to all living creatures, ourselves, the Earth, and the Universe. This is the earliest form of polytheism. But as civilizations grew, we can see a steady growth of governments using monotheism religion as a form to control the population. It is known from a psychological standpoint that humanity is more likely to act ethically correct when judged by an invisible figure they believe in, than not at all. This is not to say that religion is a fabricated story in order to control the people, for it's very likely that these deities that are worshiped today such as Jesus and Moses all actually existed at one point of time, and their story has evolved through the ages, so we use these historic figures and their life as a role model to learn from and as a tool to connect with the unseen worlds. Storytelling is a form of healing art that we have used since prehistoric time. We heal ourselves when we share our story. We learn from others, grow closer and more connected when we listen to the story of another, reminding us of our unity, that we are all connected and joined through the cosmic web of life.

If we examine religious texts we realize that we are holding tightly onto a storybook of fictional ideas and characters, with very little factual evidence of these stories ever existing, but despite the truth of whether it existed or not does not matter, because their emotions, their motives, their triumphs and failures are all real and relatable. So what do we learn from them that we cannot learn from our own story? Why do we give our power away to an outside identity instead of learning our own authenticity and improving ourselves to become the God we praise, savor, and trust? We are walking proof that life exists. We are the closest connection to God that we will ever find. Let's pause to stop searching outwards for the answers and instead focus inwards for the wisdom that we know so well.

If our soul is energy, and we know that energy never dies, what happens to our soul after we leave the Earthly plane? The religious figures who perhaps once walked this Earth, have they now evolved into Gods and Goddesses? Or have they reincarnated to live another life?

There is much debate about what happens to our soul after we die, and we can see that this very question sparked the beginning of spiritual tools and divination in modern civilizations. The earliest proof of spirituality and religion was the behavior of creating non-essential tools to support the belief of an afterlife. Non-essential tools refers to items that are not used for survival, safety, shelter, clothing, or food. This discovery is important for it shows that humankind were thinking about what happens after our time on Earth. This belief of an afterlife (whether reincarnation or heaven or hell) is a key focal point in both religion and spirituality, for it influences our decisions and experiences in our conscious world. By predicting what happens after we die, and deciding whether our actions in our life determine our life experience after death, plays a key role in how we live, hence strengthening the position of religions to play a vital role in our daily lives.

We have seen in many cases around the world that those who have had near-death experiences all had a similar experience. That is, when their heart stopped beating, they had the feeling or an actual vision of leaving their body, seeing loved ones from afar, traveling toward a light, and feeling an immense sensation of love engulfing their being. Only to then be brought back down into the Earth to learn there is more that they need to accomplish in this life. These stories are important for they emphasize the belief that the soul exists.

So, what are your beliefs? What do you think happens after we die? And how have you come to this conclusion? Is this the result of your own idea, your own research? Have you looked at all possibilities and then created your own? Your first journaling exercise for this book is to answer the question:

What happens after we die?

Soul Contract

Before your soul entered this life, it asked to elevate into a new version of itself. But you can't transform to this place by chance, you have to do the work. You need to grow through it to reach it.

In order for this transformation to take place, you will encounter many difficult challenges and the only way to truly overcome them and to evolve is to change your perception of yourself and your life. We do this through turning our awareness internally, connecting back to Source Energy, to the unseen realms where our Higher Self resides. Here in this space we are able to feed our Spiritual Self with the wisdom, support, and guidance needed to grow into different versions of ourselves, bringing forth a new vibrational frequency.

Our soul has the potential to transform into new energetic vibrations; there is no limit as to what we can create, nor what frequency we can evolve into. There is no hierarchy of evolved souls, no destination of enlightenment, for we are constantly pushing the boundaries and expanding in abundance together with the Universe. The journey of our soul's evolution is the enlightened pathway. Enlightenment is not a destination, it is the process of unlearning what we thought we knew, relearning what we already know, and remembering our true power of being connected to the cosmic energy of the Universe. You are always moving along your pathway of enlightenment because you are alive, you are living! The only way to stop this growth is by holding on to stagnant energy that keeps our vibration low, by resisting change, by not allowing our energetic vibrations to flow with life around us.

Your life purpose is to navigate this evolution of consciousness. Every challenge we are faced with offers us an invitation to push through our own imaginary limitations to change our vibrational frequency and ultimately bring the two together in harmony: the unconscious and conscious, the seen and unseen worlds. The more you learn about yourself, the more flexible you become to view your life, the easier it will be to follow your pathway to success, and the more naturally it will become to align with your soul. Although the challenges we face may sometimes feel unfair, try to hold comfort in knowing that you are supported always, for it is exactly what your soul asked for, it is the only way to grow and expand your evolution of energy, and this is the pathway to fulfilling your Soul Contract.

Your Soul Contract can be defined as the series of life lessons you are destined to encounter while living consciously on the Earthly plane. These life lessons are the very tools that will provide you with the greatest transformational growth to raise your vibrational frequency.

Before you entered this life, your soul in the unseen realms (its Higher Self form) made a decision as to the kind of life lessons you needed in order for your consciousness to evolve and expand into a higher level of awareness. The purpose of these life lessons is to enrich your experience in this lifetime, to enable personal growth, and transform the vibration of your soul. These series of life lessons are what we call your Soul Contract.

There is no time limit on completing each life lesson, and each life lesson will be repeated until the desired transformation is achieved. Sometimes this is why we experience the same challenge over and over again—because we are not learning the true message from it. And so, the same problem will continue to arise until a change to the energy of your soul's vibrational frequency has been attained, and this is usually done through an alteration to your perception of yourself and your life.

You will know when you have completed a life lesson from your Soul Contract because you will begin to see the world differently and in a more positive light. Your soul will have elevated to a higher frequency, and in this space you will feel loved and nurtured, with a strong sense of knowing. You may feel more confident in who you are, more secure in your decisions, and have more clarity from the inner voice of your Higher Self. And most importantly, you will know you have healed and mastered that life lesson for you will be able to look back upon the challenge with gratitude as it changed you in ways that you never thought possible. And now, with your new awareness of your life and confidence of self-worth, you will understand that it was that exact experience that provided you with the necessary tools to grow and transform into a new version of yourself, with a new perception of your life, thus raising the vibration of your soul's energy, the entire consciousness of the world, and bringing you closer to the abundance of love that your Higher Self emits.

The consecutive order of your life lessons vary according to the choices you make each day. You need to hold a certain understanding of the world and perception of reality in order for a particular lesson to be presented, for some lessons will only be delivered once one lesson is comprehended. The Soul Contract flows in a spiraling cycle, moving upwards or downwards. You can jump ahead of some lessons, but never go backwards. You are merely standing still if you are unable to move forward.

The series of your life lessons, your Soul Contract, is also referred to as your destiny. Your destiny implies that you have a life path, and that this life path is unable to be changed. There is truth to this idea, being that our life lessons are preconceived to ignite transformation in our soul's energy; however, we have the power to steer our life path into whatever direction we wish. And when we steer this life path we are able to bring forth an even deeper understanding, an even greater evolution of our consciousness, if we choose to do so. The chief component of this idea is change. Change is what carries us along our life path. Change is what enables transformation of our soul's energy. If we resist change, if we try to stop it, we will be in pain, for our soul needs change in order to thrive.

The context upon which each life lesson is delivered can vary greatly, and this is how we "change" the pathway of our destiny. The vibrational frequency received as the result of each life lesson remains the same, but the challenge, the situation, the circumstance upon which you are to endure this life lesson is interchangeable, based on your previous decisions. It is for this reason that there are no wrong choices in life, just a different pathway, a different order of your life lessons. Your destiny, the evolution of your soul's frequency cannot change, but the pathway to move to this place can, and that is what you have control over. You can move through each life lesson with grace and acceptance, with an open mind to see what transformation is possible, or you can resist the invitation for a new perspective, stay stagnant in your space and ultimately find yourself in pain.

resistance = pain
acceptance = peace

As we complete each life lesson of our Soul Contract we can reflect upon the negatives in our life as a positive influence, knowing that it was necessary to endure in order to attain such profound growth. And from these experiences we begin to alter our attitude toward obstacles, knowing that it is all for a higher purpose, to bring forth an enlightened perspective of our worldly experience.

From this space of acceptance and understanding we are then able to view life as "everything happens for a reason" and enjoy searching for the hidden meaning or connection between ourselves and our outer world. We learn different ways to assist us in achieving this growth through adapting our lifestyle to complement self-nurturing, self-reflection, and self-improvement.

In this book, we will explore the most common challenges that we face in our life—grief, unacceptance of our worth, inability to give and receive love, self-sabotage, heartbreak, depression, anxiety, and learn the deeper meaning behind the lessons of our Soul Contract. We will explore the reason why it exists on a soul level. And through this we will open our mind to realize that we have the ability to heal ourselves, to transform the energy of our soul, and live a happy and fulfilled life. It's all possible for you, all you need to do is learn how to align your Spiritual Self with your Higher Self, you need to align with your soul.

Life Purpose

We have awoken to realize that there is meaning to our lives and purpose to our day. But the possibilities for what we can achieve are endless and it can feel overwhelming to comprehend the depth of our true power. Often, it's easier to give that power away by entertaining the ideas of others, by choosing to support those who know their own life purpose, and so we selflessly give away our energy to support another's dream, forgetting that in order to be happy, we need to fulfill ourselves first. But how do we serve ourselves if we don't know what it is that our soul craves? By doing the work and getting to know our soul deeply. Once we learn how to listen, nurture, and honor our soul, our life purpose becomes clear to us. How? Because we feel the frequency of our energy vibration as we partake in activities and connect with others. We listen to what it is that makes us happy and we make an effort to do more of it. Moving your vibration toward what it is that brings your soul joy is the secret to living a successful life.

Your life purpose is actually quite simple—to be authentically you and to share your authenticity with the world.

To live authentically means that your actions, beliefs, and perception of the world are aligned with the voice of your soul and you do not change or adapt these according to the influences from outside sources. It's easy to be impressionable from others, especially during childhood and adolescence, when the human psyche is yet to fully develop. But as we get older and step into our own power and give ourselves permission to own our truth, we are able to dive deeply into the true vibrations of our soul to ask the questions within and self-reflect over our answers. Self-reflection then turns into self-awareness which is one of the key attributes that is needed to create the peace that we seek. There is a great lack of self-awareness in humanity due to many factors, including one's upbringing, ignorance, lack of education, and poor self-esteem. But when people are self-aware of their actions, there is less hate, less blame, less of the need for unethical and inexcusable behavior. When people are self-aware, they are living more authentically in alignment with their soul, as opposed to living in a vicious cycle of immaturity, shifting blame and playing the victim. When we live authentically we attract other like-minded individuals, and from here we build our support network of friends, leaders, teachers, and family who will encourage us to continue on our life path, fulfilling our life purpose—for this is what they are doing too. There is no jealousy, or fear of incapability, for you both know that in order to be great, you encourage others to rise with you; this is how we raise the level of consciousness of the entire world!

Living authentically means giving yourself permission to do the things that you love and the things that bring you joy. Ignore the ideas of what you should do based on society, and the pressures of others around you. What is it that you love? Where in your life do you find the most joy?

Authenticity comes hand in hand with knowing yourself, and when you know yourself you will be able to make strong decisions, have no regrets, and move through your life with ease. Let's look at the soul questions that will help build your own authenticity and self-awareness. These questions will also be good to reflect upon once you have finished this book, to see if your answers have changed after you have completed the journaling exercises for personal development.

Write down the question in your journal and reply with the first idea that comes to your mind. Allow your soul to take over your answers. Let your intuition speak.

Who am I?
Where do I come from?
What do I believe my life purpose is?
Who inspires me and why?
What do I believe in?

Once you are able to find your authentic self, the voice of your soul will speak louder and you will be able to understand how to share your gift with the world.

We refer to your authentic gift as your medicine, because medicine is able to heal, and your gift does exactly that—by being you, you are healing the world and raising the vibrational frequency. This is how important you are! You are here for a great divine purpose, not only to fulfill your Soul Contract and raise your own vibration, but to raise the vibrational frequency of the whole world, the whole Universe. And you do this simply by being your authentic self.

The question still remains: what is your medicine? What is your great gift to share with the world? If we cannot find the answer to this, we will feel at a loss with our life, emptiness in our day, and a lack of connection with ourselves and the world around us. Finding a purpose in our life is crucial to personal fulfillment. And the answer to find this starts with the simple question of "what is it that makes me happy?"

But such a simple question brings forth great confusion, because we are overwhelmed with endless possibilities, or limiting beliefs that make us think that we aren't good enough. Those limitations can arrive in the forms of pressure from others' opinions around us, pressure of society's need for consumerism in order to thrive, and pressure from ourselves. But the heaviest burden of all? Money. Either the cost to educate ourselves about our chosen talent is unaffordable, or the money received if we were to excel in such a task is not viable to live off. And so, we are constantly putting aside our true desires because the pressures of society to buy a house, get an education, provide for families, and look after the basic necessities for survival are too stressful. But this is the pressure we place upon ourselves too to reach these goals. But are these your goals or that of another?

Imagine if we lived in a world where money was not a factor for survival. If we were free to share our talents and passions with each other, sharing the love of what brings us true joy with nothing needed to be exchanged except for the experience of connection with one another? Would there be enough curious minds in the world to look after every element of the Earth? We will never know because we are encouraged to live like sardines amidst a tin can of wealth and greed. Unable to be free to do as we truly wish. But these limitations are also part of a great imaginative web that we play our role in. For if the power was not given, power would not be received. If you are willing to look outside the perimeters that are handed to you, you will find the sweet success that you crave. All you need to do is dare to dream, believe, and seek the answers that you wish.

When you choose to share your own medicine know that the Universe will support you wholeheartedly. For when you listen to the cravings of your soul, and move your vibration toward this space, you will align with your Higher Self, and remember—from this place, anything is possible. This is the space where you manifest your destiny.

But how do we find out what our true passion is? How does one discover the truth of their medicine? To answer this, we're going to get creative and practical. Get your journal out and ask yourself the following questions:

What did I love doing as a child before the world told me not to?
What areas of my life do I succeed at naturally?
If I asked three close friends what they thought I did best, or how they would describe me, what would they say?
What do I love to share with others?
What does success mean to me?
What does the world need that I can give?

From this list, compile some business ideas and try them out. Educate yourself, research, and experiment! We learn through trial and error. And although one idea may not work out, it will evolve and flow toward the truth of what it is that you are meant to be doing with your life.

When you figure out your unique medicine for the world you may be tested to prove that it's truly what you want. You may go through difficult times, and yet you have been taught that life should be flowing if you are following your Soul Contract, right? Just because your life isn't flowing the way it is meant to doesn't mean that you are on the wrong path. If you have figured out what you truly love doing, and what brings you the most passion in the world you need to persevere against all odds. Only though the darkest times can you find the brightest light, and with time and dedication you will taste the sweet success of your fruitful labor and it will be the most euphoric high of your life!

Finding our life purpose isn't the end result of our journey. We also need to move through the challenges and experiences to evolve and develop our awareness. But how do we continuously find the strength to show up and face the challenges of every day? How do we handle the harsh truths of reality that we are faced with? We turn that outward question back into ourselves and journey deep within to seek the truth.

In order to find the answers that we seek, we need to harmonize the flow of energy between our mind, body, and soul. We do this by understanding the abundance of energies that surround us. The more we learn how to self-soothe our energy field with these Universal Energies, the clearer our connection with our Higher Self becomes, the louder the voice of our intuition rises, and the more power we will hold to steer our life toward the direction that we wish.

Spiritual Philosophy

According to the Quantum Field Theory, at the core of every living manifested consciousness lies an energy force. This belief can be traced back to ancient transcripts in every country around the world where we see a strict dedication to deities and god-like entities for every spiritual force. But, aside from knowing this on a scientific level, we also believe this from our own connection with every living creature. We know two important things about energy:

1. Energy never dies; it continuously transforms into something different.

2. Energy exists in abundance without limits, meaning that we can tap into other energy fields at all times.

These two components of energy are the fundamental factors behind spiritual philosophy.

Spiritual philosophy is a combination of beliefs, ideas, and practices based off nature, knowledge, and experience that focus on harmonizing the flow of energy between our mind, body, and soul. This in turn nurtures and supports our emotional wellbeing thus enabling us to create a meaningful life. To better understand this, let's look at the three key attributes of spiritual philosophy:

Spiritual Philosophy #1
Everything is connected.
Our perception of life relies heavily upon the connection we believe to exist between our internal self (our soul) and the outside world (other energetic entities). When we shift our outlook on life from "me" to

"we," we are able to feel the connection of every living creature around us. We learn through our experience that we are indeed a part of the cosmic Universe. From feeling this connection of energy we then redefine our life journey, values, and beliefs. We realize that our life experiences are more rewarding when we share it with others. By promoting a sense of unity amongst everyone around us we create peace between us, eliminating the fear of being alone. The more time we spend honoring these connections with all living creatures, both people, and animal and plant life, the greater rewards we receive in return. We are then able to derive a valuable life experience which provides fulfillment to our lives through a sense of belonging. Our perception of life constantly changes because energy is always transforming.

Spiritual Philosophy #2

Everything is energy.

A spiritual person believes and understands that all living creatures (including ourselves) are made of energy. For this reason, spiritual philosophy focuses on cleansing, revitalizing, rejuvenating, and harnessing energy. Examples of this can be done through meditations, or drawing strength from Mother Nature's natural resources. When you apply a spiritual outlook to your life, you understand that everything circles as one, a never-ending cycle of energy. We have the power to create, manipulate, and disconnect from unseen energy to steer our life into the direction that we desire. By aligning ourselves with our chosen vibration we are taking control of our own destiny.

Spiritual Philosophy #3

We are an eternal spirit evolving through life experiences.

Spirituality encourages the observer to continuously evolve their own awareness of consciousness from the realms of unconsciousness. Through the practice of gratitude, love, awareness, compassion, and understanding, we can heal, forgive, and move forward on our life path. Allowing life to flow around us, as opposed to drowning amongst it. Through transforming this energy, we encourage the idea that we are in fact the creators of our world, our own Godly existence, and from this point of view, spirituality empowers the observer to make their own decisions, accepting that life is flowing with one purpose and that is to fulfill our Soul Contract.

As we learn more about ourselves and the role we play with spirituality, we embark on a quest of personal development. Through this development we are faced with challenges that contain, but are not limited to, combating limiting beliefs, healing our inner child, confronting our ego, and false identities. As we conquer each challenge we develop self-awareness and emotional intelligence which are crucial components to assist us on our journey of self-discovery.

All challenges and triumphs, both negative and positive experiences, are all connected and assist in the evolution of our internal spirit to reach a higher level of consciousness. This is achieved through the discovery of profound wisdom revealed in accordance to the "Divine Time" (the pathway of our destiny). Throughout our lives we explore trial and error as we lean into aligning ourselves with who it is that we believe we are and what it is we are meant to become (our life purpose).

But in order to understand who it is that we are meant to become, we need to understand who we are, and the best way to do this is to look at the creator of everything—ourselves, the Universe, and life as we know it. We need to begin with Universal Energy.

When we thoroughly understand Universal Life-Force Energy we learn how to nurture our own vibrational frequency so that we may evolve through our life. This is a key attribute linked to spiritual philosophy.

The more you explore your own energy field and that of the world around you, the clearer this belief that energy is our life force becomes. We can see it from the simple comparison between our body when we are sick versus when we are healthy, as our ability to do things becomes staggered and difficult. Just like our body needs a detox and cleanse, so too does our mind and soul. We can always harmonize the flow of our energy using natural resources that are available to us, we just need to remember how.

As we tap into the infinite wisdom of knowing that "everything is energy," we are reminded that this is the core basis from where our reality evolved from. Our attitude, reaction, and perception of life, relies on our ability to understand energy. For when our energy is exhausted, tired, or stressed, we view the world in a particular lens. When our energy is revitalized, released, and that of a higher vibrational frequency, we are in love with life and are open to receiving its blessings. It's not possible to stay on only one side, and the reason why is because we need the opposite in order to define what one is, to provide meaning and understanding. If something isn't hot, it's cold, it's either wet or dry, soft or hard. The polar opposites are required in order to derive meaning from each other, and yet at the same time they are as one, a unified energetic frequency when neutralized. It is us who brings forth meaning to them.

Spiritual philosophy entails that we are experiencing life through the lens of our eternal soul. And that this lens, our perception of life, is altered based on our life experiences and internal beliefs. Our Soul

Contract consists of a series of life lessons whose sole purpose is to encourage transformation of that perception, with its ultimate goal to bring you into alignment with your Higher Self (your soul in the unseen realms). You are always connected to your Higher Self, but the energy when moving between the two worlds of consciousness and unconsciousness clouds your feeling and vision. You forget what it is like to be at one with the Universe. If you remembered this truth your life would become easier for you would remember that you are divinely guided at all times, that you have the power within to create the world that you wish. With every challenge that we overcome the energy of our soul transforms and raises itself higher.

Knowing that we have the power to heal ourselves and that by doing so will take us further along the spiral staircase of our evolution brings us confidence, for we are able to take control of our life, and cease to play the victim. We can then apply the second element of spiritual philosophy that "everything is connected," and from here we realize that it is not just "me" in this world, struggling to fit in, but we are "we" co-creating our life together. Every person and situation is placed in our life for a reason. We have chosen to take this task on together, and when we remind ourselves of this, we can learn how to use this tool to further our own personal development and encourage a positive transformation of evolution within us and the world around us.

If everything is energy, then all we need to do is learn how to harness, release, cleanse, and rejuvenate this energy. And when you learn how to do this, you can apply this technique to everything. Pain, grief, anger is all energy, so when we release, we heal and we transform this energy into wisdom. The more we learn how to be an alchemist for energy to transform within and around us, the more pleasurable our life will be, the easier it will be to live in the present moment and see things for what they really are.

To summarize this section of "Understanding Our Soul," I'd like to reiterate a few key points, for we will be referring to them often throughout the book.

1) Our soul is made of energy and this energy lives in the seen and unseen worlds as our Spiritual Self and Higher Self. We connect these two "worlds" together through our intuition and unconsciousness.

2) The unseen worlds is our unconscious energy that cannot be defined for if it is defined it will move into the seen worlds (into our reality).

3) Our soul, reality, and unconsciousness are all connected to the never-ending fabric of Universal Energy. This energy is constantly transforming, evolving, and expanding.

4) To live a fulfilled life of love, passion, and healing light, we need to work with the energy of our soul and transform this energy into new vibrations to support our ultimate evolution.

Our soul exists in both places, the seen and unseen worlds, but when our soul "lives" in the seen worlds, in our reality, as our Spiritual Self, in human form, we tend to forget about ourselves in the unseen worlds. For our attention is completely absorbed with survival, with living, with connecting to others in a different way. We have a body, a mind, emotions, challenges, and obstacles to overcome. Whereas our soul in the unseen worlds is vibrating in a high frequency where these low feelings of sadness, grief, and fear do not exist. One of the greatest life lessons and the most important in order for our journey to evolve on Earth is to recognize this fact: that we are a soul dancing between the worlds of the seen and unseen.

Of these beliefs, take what resonates with you. You may find that you have had experiences of supernatural occurrences that help shape your own belief system to be similar. However, there are some people in this world who have never encountered a soulful connection, who have never witnessed a supernatural experience and therefore, they do not believe that the soul exists. And that's their journey, not mine. Let them be and let them learn on their own when the time is right. I know that it feels hard when faced with challenging people who are the complete opposite to who you are and what you stand for. You wonder how they could come into your life? How could people exist with such turmoil and negativity in their hearts? And furthermore, why do you need to meet them? Remember, we are all evolving at different rates. We are becoming conscious in different periods of our lives. Some people become conscious at birth; others, not until just before their death. Whenever the time is right for you it will happen; don't try to rush it, don't try to predetermine when it is. Just trust that whatever is happening is meant to happen, because this is your Soul Contract and everything is right on time.

Now that you have a thorough understanding of the core principles of spiritual philosophy, the energy of our soul, and the connection of our Higher Self in the unseen worlds, let's look at the natural resources that surround us. When we know how to call upon these resources we learn how to harmonize the energy flow between our mind, body, and soul, thus providing us with the courage we need to steer our life path along the direction that we wish, to provide us with a deeply meaningful life.

Nurture thy Soul

Balanced. Calm. Supported. Nurtured. In love with the Universe.
I wandered through the fields of dirt and broken shadows to find true love.
And there it was ... But not a person, not an object or a creature, it was an
energy. It was the source of creation. And in this space of beauty and wisdom
I asked her to heal me, to love me. And I threw myself carelessly into the
wildness of her arms. Dancing with freedom around the space I felt at home.
The stones and fire dispersed before me, I saw the energy that they provided,
the essence of their beauty. It was within me and around me. I didn't want to
leave. I didn't want to stop. It was the first time in my life that I felt complete
wholeness. It was the first time in my life that I felt truly alive.

Universal Energy

The belief of Universal Energy can be traced back to the Indigenous tribes of pre-civilization. Within these communities a leader would be appointed who held the strongest connection with the energies of the Universe, therefore holding the power to pave the pathway to a greater future. He or she was referred to as the Shaman, Sorcerer, or Witch, for they had the ability to recognize the Universal Energy in the unseen worlds and bring it forth into the collective consciousness.

The traditions of their knowledge and techniques have been handed down through the generations via word of mouth and hands-on practice. The Witch, Sorcerer, and Shaman of the Indigenous tribes are the ones who understand the true wisdom of the soil, sunshine, rain, and entire eco-system and for this reason, they are the people who know how to save our planet. They are the wisest humans in the world for they have mastered the connection between the two worlds from the sacred knowledge that has been accumulated since the beginning of time. When the next apprentice is taught the wisdom of the Universe, an initiation takes place to signal their graduation and the tradition continues.

But over time, as civilizations grew, the idea that Shamans and Witches could become more powerful than humanity did not sit well with those who wished to rule the world. They were competing with a series of rules and regulations that they did not choose, that were chosen for them, that had been collected over the life paths of many tribes around the world. And so, in order to hold the power unanimously they needed the people to fear and become dependent on their services. Through colonization and by focusing on one religion with one God it was easier to control the population. And with these new ideas of a monotheism God came the reliance of the people upon the church and state. No more did the people know they had the power within to create their own life, no more did they give themselves permission to live as they wished. The governments, kings, and queens had control over the people and were able to create a hierarchy of fictional titles in a pyramid that ensured the division of different classes could be established and respected.

Imagine what would happen to the world if the people were able to wake up and realize the abundance of their own power? Not only realize, but actually use this power to benefit themselves, their loved ones and the entire consciousness of the world? We would be able to live a healthier life in greater harmony, as we learn the truth that Mother Earth provides us with everything we need to live a fulfilled life. We would be able to assist in balancing the energy of the planet, for no more would we mass produce products, whether cattle, or coal, for greed, money, or power. We would remember that we are gifted with all the elements to create a happy life around us right in this moment. We have fresh water to nurture our bodies and emotions, we have natural medicine from the plants to nourish and strengthen our physical self, our immunity, and we could rely on solar energy to support the electrical needs for warmth and light. Although electricity and water are able to be free resources available to us, the leaders have taken this power as a form of control. We are pushed to believe that our bodies aren't strong enough to survive and we are encouraged to put unnatural substances into our body, ignoring the fact that we are capable of healing ourselves when we change our environment internally and externally.

But we are restricted to form our own opinion due to the control that has been established over the years through technological monitoring. We are restricted to start a conversation questioning the platter we have been handed due to strict laws and legalities in place. There are also people who believe that to question our society is evil, and therefore to know who you can speak with about how to change the world is becoming more and more difficult. We must not despair and continue to seek the like-minded individuals to share information with and to raise our concerns without prejudice or criticism, but instead find those who listen with curiosity and sage advice. We need to resort to the original ways of gathering knowledge and information —through word of mouth and hands-on techniques. Even though it appears we are able to reach wider audiences through the advancement of technology, our every move is monitored under strict control, through investigation, without any room for questioning the rules. But the consciousness of the world is awakening and we are realizing our duty on Earth is not to live and serve others, for this is not sustainable. Together we will learn, remember, and we will rise.

But until that day comes we need to prepare ourselves with the way of the Shaman, the way of the Witch and Sorcerer; we need to gather our own practices as to what makes us feel good, what empowers us, and from here, we teach the next generation to come. We are remembering what it is to be powerful within, we are learning to heal ourselves with magical potions—herbs and plant medicines—with energy healing work—such as meditation, reiki, sound vibrations—as we harness the Universal Energies that surround us.

When we learn how to nourish our soul we will become clearer in our mind, more courageous in our stance, and the answers of how to survive become simplified. For we will know how to give love back to the Earth, to the Universe, and this is through remembering we are all connected. What we do to ourselves and others is reflected in the Earth and will come back full circle. We do this by learning how to cleanse and revitalize our energy fields with the aid of plant medicines, potions, and rituals. The more we practice connecting with the energy from our perceived reality and the energy from the spiritual realms, the more we will be able to influence great change into our lives. Just as the spirit elders of Indigenous tribes teach—the key to a long-lasting life of health and prosperity relies heavily on harnessing this spiritual energy.

There are five primary sources of Universal Energy: Fire, Earth, Air, Water, and Aether (space). We can trace these five identities across the world, in every form of religious practice, and we can learn our own truth to their existence through our own rituals that we choose to embark upon. Ancient Wicca and Pagan Witchcraft traditions harness these energies to create rituals and spells to support their goals and dreams. Shamans harnessed this energy through plant medicines, journeying into the unseen world to bring the messages from our ancestors and spirit guides into our waking life to navigate our life path with depth and ease.

As we explore the following energies, ask yourself what they mean to you. Questions such as:

What does this energy gift me?
How do I feel when I am with this energy?
Which energy do I feel most connected to?
If the energy was to provide me with a message, what would it be?

You can also learn about your connection with Universal Energy in relation to your horoscope, as there are many people who resonate with the energy of the birth sign that they are born into. I myself am an Earth sign, and this is truly where I feel the most replenished. The more you practice working with these energies, the more natural it will be for you to call upon their wisdom.

Earth Energy

Surrender wholeheartedly into her love.
Feel the weight of her existence upon your skin
and with delicate kisses she will heal your pain,
soothe your fears and answer your prayers.

Earth Energy has incredible nurturing power to heal the vibrational frequency of your being. There's a reason that the Earth is called Mother Nature, for she is the creator of life. Our bodies are an extension of nature. We have mountains and rivers just like the Earth. Our veins represent the roots of the tree, or the crackling lines of dried mud near a waterfall. We are intertwined with every element of nature. Without Her, we cannot exist. We talk about the need to protect the environment, to save Mother Nature, but the truth is, it's not she who needs saving—it's us. She will continue to exist with or without our life. She has withstood great transformation since the beginning of time—billions and billions of years. And even though, it is debated as to how life came into existence (or perhaps more so, the purpose of life)—what we do know is that Mother Nature was the beginning and she will be the end. When she finishes, we finish. We cannot survive without her love. Yet, even if a grand explosion erupts from the sky and destroys everything, she will rebuild, reshape, and live again. We, however, may not.

The support that Earth Energy provides as it nurtures our soul is due to the fact that her energy is the original creator; by touching her, we connect back into the source from where it is that we came from. Engraved in her existence is the history of our ancestors, and so, we connect through to our roots with the help of her memory. She holds ancient wisdom that has the ability to teach us how to self-heal and navigate our life path with ease. And the simple touch of dirt to our skin has the ability to ground our souls into our body, reminding us of who we really are. A large problem with mental health today is that it is a form of our soul not wanting to be in our body and living in reality. To help heal this pain we can learn how to cleanse and replenish our energy through grounding techniques with Mother Nature.

What do you imagine when you think about the ground? Perhaps you think of dirt, leaves, trees, bark, or rocks? What can you smell? The scents of the rainforest? Maybe rain or moss? When we practice grounding ourselves, that's where we need to go—back to where it all began. Immerse yourself into nature. Touch the rocks with your bare feet, feel the grass beneath your skin, and massage the dirt into the soles of your feet. Don't just stand and absorb—sit down, lie down, and relax. Allow the magic of the ground beneath you to connect you back into where it is that you came from. Use the following spiritual technique to harness Earth Energy:

Grounding Through Mother Nature

Nature is one of the strongest tools you can use to ground yourself. The simple act of walking barefoot on the Earth and feeling the dirt between your toes and on the soles of your feet can ground your soul back into your body in a swift heartbeat.

1) Go to your closest source of Mother Nature that is connected to the Earth. This could be your backyard, a rainforest, park, beach, or natural landmark.

2) Take off your shoes, stand or lie down with your skin touching the dirt and feel the energy of the ground beneath you, nurturing your body.

3) Inhale and exhale gently as you allow yourself to become heavy and completely supported by Mother Nature.

4) In this space, set your intention: "I receive nurturing vibrations from Mother Nature/ Earth Energy as she grounds my soul into my body."

5) Feel the sensation of her life on your skin, and remind yourself how deeply supported and loved you are as you feel her touch.

6) Close your eyes and imagine your feet or pelvis growing roots like a tree deep into the ground. Imagine these roots as colored light energy moving through the layers of the Earth into the core, where molten lava resides. Imagine yourself traveling through the roots into the energy field of the center of the Earth.

7) Connect deeper to this energy by imagining the temperature, the texture, the colors, anything that supports your imagination of harnessing these beautiful vibrations.

8) Imagine the nurturing love from Mother Nature moving up through these cords of light energy and sending you healing strength. Feel yourself become even heavier as your energy roots sink deeper into the ground, immersed in Mother Nature. Give yourself permission to receive her love.

9) Continue this cycle of energy of giving and receiving with Mother Nature. Stay in this space for as long as you need, until you start

to see things differently. Allow any visions to play out before you, and trust the messages that arise.

Continue exploring the gifts of Mother Nature by using whatever you can see around you. Are there flowers? Touch their petals, smell their scent and stare at the beauty of their colors. Maybe you have a cactus? Feel the sharpness of its prickle and the sponginess of its skin; it's tough on the outside, but inside, it's just soft mush. The leaves on the ground, notice the way they crunch under your skin, hear the sound and smell the aroma of Earth around you.

Touch, feel and allow the sensation of life to cocoon you with love as you naturally release any stress that you feel in your body and give it to Mother Nature as you stand or lie down upon the soil. She is able to take away any pain that you may feel.

With regular practice of this grounding technique, your mind will be able to clear any unnecessary thoughts with ease. You will find yourself living in the present moment as you watch the gentle breeze move over the grass by your feet or in the leaves of the trees above. And from this space you will be mesmerized by the simple movement of life breathing.

Grounding Mantras:
I am safe.
I am nurtured.
I trust my pathway.
I am grounded in my soul.
I am open to new discoveries.
The Earth is always healing me.
I feel the strength of my ancestors beside me.
I surrender with great knowing that all is as it should be.

Water Energy

I dive deeply into the stream of blessed water.
Allowing my thoughts to float by, she reminds me to stay strong.
She teaches me that softness isn't weakness,
for her currents can be gentle yet they have the power to move land.

Water Energy represents our emotional wellbeing. Our emotions have the ability to change and flow into extreme directions. They have the ability to raise our energy vibrations up high or drown ourselves completely into deep darkness. The more we learn to look at our emotions as Water Energy, the easier it will become to cleanse, revitalize and let them flow. Our emotions and feelings are the result of our thoughts about a situation, or an attachment to a situation. Although we can learn how to control our thoughts through the practice of meditation, sometimes our emotions burst without our consent. This is when we look to Water Energy.

We receive an abundance of nutrients and minerals from drinking and bathing in water, which in turn refreshes our senses and cleanses our energy levels. When we immerse ourselves in water it replicates the memory of being inside our mother's womb. Here in this space we are safe and nurtured, and therefore the same results are achieved. This aids the growth of our emotional intelligence as well because when we allow our emotions to subside we can self-reflect. From a scientific standpoint, our body is made up of 60 - 70% water; for this reason, Water Energy is able to not only soothe our emotions but replenish and revitalize our energy, thus supporting our spiritual psyche to transmute into a higher level of awareness.

Nurturing Emotions With Water Energy

Nurturing our emotions with Water Energy can be done in several ways, such as having a shower or bath, swimming in the ocean, or hydrating our internal organs by drinking water. Whatever you choose, ensure that your body comes into contact with the water, and then use visualization to encourage transformation.

1) Connect with the Water Energy, whether it be internally (drinking water) or externally (showering, bathing, swimming).

2) Imagine the Water Energy as a nourishing light full of love. This loving light energy has the ability to remove stagnant emotional disturbances in your energy field as you allow the water to wash over your skin or hydrate your body from the inside out.

3) As you come into contact with the water, imagine your energy being cleansed and revitalized. Envision your energy being removed and replaced with beautiful loving light energy from the water.

For example, if you are showering, focus on each droplet of water as it splashes onto your body and imagine that it is pushing any stagnant energy out of you. If you are bathing, envision the line between your body and the water to disappear. Let yourself become one with the water; it is as though you are floating amongst the fabrics of time and surrendering all of your problems into this field of non-existence. Allow the water to cleanse and refresh your body, in turn nurturing and nourishing the energy of your soul.

Air Energy

I say the word peace and as the sound echoes in my heart,
my vibration is soothed—I feel at one with the Universe.
With every breath in and every breath out
I surrender my fears, as the Divine holds me gracefully,
and within this space, I know I am loved by the Universe.

Air is the life force energy behind every living creature on this Earth. Without air we cease to exist. Our body continues to breathe regardless of our doing or thinking. Yet when we focus our attention on using our breath to support our wellbeing we are able to enter a stage of deep meditation, providing us with profound insight into our darkest problems. Air is our greatest tool for survival. Using a variety of techniques, our breath enables a smooth passageway into the realm of unconsciousness. It is here that we are able to recall past lives, connect with outer realms, and heal our trauma as we create peace and tranquility within our mind, body, and perceived reality. Air provides us with the gift of clarity as it supports powerful transformation within us. The words we speak are created with Air Energy and therefore, air is a symbol of communication. The vibrational tones we can create through our words have the power to heal, connect, nurture, and provide love to ourselves and others. We can speak our intentions clearly and recite manifestations and mantras into the Universe, enabling our lives to change. Air influences the weather in our atmosphere into calmness or chaos, and this is reflected in ourselves too. Air cleanses our internal organs, removes toxins and impurities from our system. Air enables all forms of life to circulate on this planet; without it we cannot survive.

How to Use Your Breath to Calm Yourself

Air Energy can be harnessed by taking deep breaths in and out very slowly to create deep peace within yourself. All you need to do is exhale for at least a second longer than you inhale.

Try it with me below:

Inhale for 1, 2, 3, 4.

Exhale for 1, 2, 3, 4, 5.

Repeat this for a minimum of three breaths and until you feel your presence calm down.

Take it one step further, and with each breath in, imagine that you are breathing in beautiful, loving vibrations. And as you breathe out, imagine you are releasing any energy that you do not need.

The more we practice breathing slowly and properly, the easier meditations become and the more mindfulness we can invite into our day. Try to incorporate three to five deep breaths in every day (morning and evening), and see how different you feel.

Fire Energy

Mesmerized by his flames, the fire within my soul blazes too.
I honor your path with gratitude, you inspire the power within me.
I, too, can destruct; I, too, can create; I, too, can transform.

The illuminated flame of the fire reminds us of the divine light within us, the pure, loving energy of our Higher Self. This light energy provides us with hope in dark times, for only against the darkest backdrop is the light able to shine so bright. The fire is a true representation of honoring both the light and dark within ourselves and the world around us. The warmth from Fire Energy brings us nurturing peace whilst the smell, sound, and sight erupts a mixture of emotion—both calming and yet invigorating. At the core center of our planet there are blazing flames, signalizing the creation of energy; this fire mirrors the divine light of energy within our soul. Just as fire enables creation, it also promotes destruction and transformation. And from these three elements the cycle of life is born. Create, transform, destruct, transform, create. Just as all energy is renewed, our emotions and challenges in life move with the same ebb and flow of the Universe; it comes full circle back to the beginning yet with fresh ideas, new perspective, only to transform and die and be born again.

Fire can be viewed as an armor to protect ourselves, our heart, our loved ones, for nothing can withstand the burning flames. The light of fire ignites creative ideas, influencing knowledge and governing the business side of our life. Candles are lit to symbolize life as well as death, celebrations, and relaxed environments. In each scenario the purpose of the flame is to align our mind with the present moment, connecting us back to Source Energy, our Higher Self in the unseen worlds.

Nurturing our soul with Fire Energy can be achieved through simply lighting a candle. As we stare at the flame and connect to the source of beauty that breathes life, we are able to calm our mind into a place of peace, acceptance, and understanding. Just as the flame represents death and rebirth, we too are able to spark ideas within ourselves. You may use the flame of a candle to let go of stagnant thoughts, fears, or limiting beliefs, and call upon the same energy to ignite fresh ideas and loving vibrations.

Harnessing Fire Energy for Transformation

1. Get into a meditative state by slowing down your breathing.

2. Close your eyes and imagine a flame of fire inside you or in front of you. Take your time imagining this fire. Envision the textures, the colors and size. Feel the warmth of this fire.

3. This is your fire of creation, destruction and transformation. What do you wish to do? If you wish to create, imagine what you wish to create and see it in the fire. Allow the energy to grow and bring forth inspiration. If you wish to transform, feed the energy you wish to release into the flames. Let the energy be destructed and transformed into new vibrations.

Remember this fire within you is always blazing. Close your eyes and imagine this flame whenever you find yourself needing strength, courage, or protection.

Aether/ Spirit Energy

I foresee my dreams and now I walk boldly through
the gate of non-resistance, to enter wholeheartedly
into a space of love, of utter bliss.

Aether is the leader of the Universal Energy family, for it allows each element to expand and display their gifts, and therefore is the backdrop for creation to exist.

If we examine the connection of the elements together we can also see how each element either raises the other up, or destroys it down. For fire to exist, it needs air to breathe and Earth (something tangible to burn); these two equal a harmonizing relationship. But water can suffocate the fire, the same way that fire (heat), evaporates the water; therefore, water and fire are not compatible. For Earth to flourish it needs water and air to grow. Air relies on water and Earth to continue circulating. Balance is needed for each energy to thrive.

Aether is the almighty powerful element of the five for without it, the other four are non-existent. We also refer to Aether as Spirit Energy in our rituals, for Spirit Energy is the creator of all matter, yet exists purely in the realm of unconsciousness. Just as the unseen realms cannot be defined, the energy of spirit knows no boundaries. With Spirit Energy, anything is possible. We can create, destroy, harness, release; everything is possible.

Spirit Energy is the most powerful representation of Gods and Goddesses across all religions and beliefs. It is the substance to life, for every living creature in the Universe has a Spirit Energy within it. Spirit Energy is the core of our soul energy too; we have Spirit Energy within our soul, so when asking for Spirit Energy to bless us, we are speaking to ourselves, and the energy from the unseen worlds. These five elements create consciousness.

It's important to have a basic understanding of the Universal Energy in order to live a balanced life. We use this energy to cleanse, recharge, and replenish our own energy field daily, with or without our awareness. But if we learn to recognize each of the elements as we encounter them and honor the gift that they bring, we will nurture our soul with more depth and harmonize the flow of energy between our mind, body, and soul.

Because we and everything is made of energy, understanding how to work with Universal Energy is extremely important in our life journey. If you learn how to harness the essence of each of these energies you will find the solution to heal any area of your life.

We will explore how to apply each energy in various spiritual practices as we journey through this book together. Let's first start with the most important energy techniques to learn—how to cleanse, protect, and recharge our energy.

Cleansing Your Energy

Energy acts like a magnet with other energy; they like to conjoin together. Most often, like-minded energy attracts like-minded energy. This is the basis as to why it's important to be aware of the energy you are emitting to ensure that you are projecting the right kind of energy you wish to receive in return. But what happens if you come into contact with negative energy, even though you are radiating beautiful positive vibrations? The negative energy is also attracted to your higher frequencies and will try to stick to you, in an attempt to raise its own vibration up higher, yet while doing so, it is depleting you of your own energy. It's for this reason that it's important to cleanse and protect our energy often in order to rejuvenate and revitalize our own energy field. We need to practice letting go of vibrations that serve us no good, that hold us back from being our true selves. How can you expect to harness new energy if you are holding on to darkness?

There are many tools you can adapt into your lifestyle to cleanse your energy field, to take back your power. There are no rules as to how often you should cleanse and rejuvenate your energy; what you need to do is take note of how you feel and recognize the signs that your body, mind, and soul is in need of a reset and a recharge.

Common signs that tell you it is time to cleanse your energy:
• You feel drained and exhausted.
• You feel heavy, confused, and unable to make decisions.
• Your digestion is blocked.
• You feel aches in your body.
• You feel irritated and angry.

How to Cleanse Your Energy

Before cleansing your energy, it's important to identify where in your body you are holding stagnant energy, or where the dark energy is clinging to you.

To do this, close your eyes and say:
Show me where I am holding trapped energy.
Show me where there is dark energy stuck to me.
Show me where in my body I need cleansing.

Move your awareness through to various areas of your body and allow your soul to show you the areas where this energy is stuck. Use your intuition and sense of feeling to identify this energy. Start from your feet and move your way up through to the crown of your head.

Close your eyes and ask yourself:
Where in my body feels heavy?

Once you recognize the area ask more questions:
What color is this energy? i.e. black, blue, brown.
What texture is this energy? i.e. thin, runny, chunky.
What is the weight of this energy? i.e. light, heavy.

By this stage you should have a clear image of the weight, color, and texture of the energy that is trapped in your aura. You may feel or see one or all of the descriptions; what is most important is identifying the sensation where you feel blocked, heavy, or stagnant.

Once we have identified the energy we wish to remove, let's move onto the following practices to cleanse this energy.

1. Breath Work and Intention (Air Energy)

Use your intention:

"I am releasing, removing, cleansing this energy with my breath."

After you have identified where the stagnant energy is, envision the energy being removed with deep breaths in and out. An example of this can be to see your breath as a light that is pushing the energy out of your energy field. Imagine the feeling of the energy being released and allow yourself to feel lighter.

2. Move Your Body (Aether Energy)

Use physical movement to release stagnant energy within your aura. This can be through exercise, dancing, jumping, or shaking. Do it consistently for at least 15 - 30 minutes so that your energy is given the opportunity to be released. You may feel a sense of "buzzing" energy from within as the stale energy is moved out of your space.

3. Burn White Sage (Air + Fire Energy)

White sage is an ancient tool used by Indigenous tribes around the world to cleanse energy in a sacred ritual known as "smudging." This tradition dates back centuries and is now a popular modern form of cleansing as it is so potent that it removes the darkest energy, purifying it with ease. Ensure all windows are open and that you are nowhere near the elderly, children, or people with breathing problems. Burn the edge of the bundle of dried sage leaves, and blow the flame out. Move the smoke over the area you wish to cleanse and use your intention. The smoke from white sage is scientifically proven to remove impurities and toxins in the atmosphere.

4. Sound Energy (Air Energy)

All energy holds a level of vibrational frequencies; negative energy is of the lowest frequency possible, so we can overrule this vibration or eliminate it completely by using a high vibrational frequency. What better frequency is there than sound! Sound removes dark energy using the tones of high vibrational frequencies. Good tools for this are chimes, gongs, bells, or any musical instrument. Simply singing is also another way to clear the energy too.

The following is a creative visualization technique that will assist you in cleansing any stagnant or negative energy that is attached to you.

Removing Negative Energy With Visualization

1. Close your eyes, get into a comfortable position (lying down is good for this particular exercise, but you can also sit up if you prefer).

2. Set your intention: "To cleanse negative energy from my aura."

3. Enter your meditation for about 5 - 10 minutes and when ready, imagine you are lying upon a golden net and at each edge of the golden net there is an angelic beings holding the net beneath you. These angelic entities could be angels, spirit guides, loved ones who have passed. They are holding the net beneath you.

4. Ask for help from these angelic beings to cleanse your energy and then envision the golden net moving through your body slowly.

5. As the net passes through your body, envision it pulling and extracting any negative vibrations that are caught in your energy field. Breathe deeply, surrendering any stagnant energy in your aura. Repeat this process as needed.

Protecting Your Energy

We are always in a continuous cycle of reciprocating energy and it's up to us to ensure that our energy exchange is equal. There are two ways that your energy can be affected by other people. One is through an energy leak, and the other is when we absorb other people's negative energy.

An energy leak is when someone takes more energy from you than what they give in return. You know when this happens to you for you will feel strangely exhausted and drained after spending time with someone. You may even have been partaking in an activity that usually brings you joy but instead you feel as though all your energy has been sucked out. This is a form of your energy leaking. Beautiful light and loving energy is attractive, and it is not unusual for another person to be drawn to you, wanting more and more. But take note when this happens; become aware that the energy exchange is unbalanced and reserve your energy. If you do not receive an equal exchange of value when spending time with someone, choose to spend your time with someone who can reciprocate your own energy. Always listen to yourself. If you feel like someone's energy is not serving your best interests, don't ignore that feeling, and act upon it. Distance yourself from them.

Another way our energy is depleted is through encounters with people who have negative energies and we absorb those low vibrations and carry them around with us unaware. When this happens you might feel strange symptoms such as difficulty swallowing, a headache or a sense of displacement. Irritation and anger are also symptoms of being near dark energies, and unknowingly you will be taking on their own problems from being near them. When this happens you have already absorbed the negative energy, and so you will need to cleanse your energy also. I will show you a good tool to use in the following exercise. Remember —you can use these techniques at any point of the day, even while interacting with the negative energy. Sometimes we are confronted with dark energies with little choice to remove ourselves from it, perhaps through work or even relatives that move at a different frequency to you. You can still interact with these energies, but protect yourself, cleanse yourself, and recharge your energy to stay grounded and balanced in harmony.

Even though these occurrences sound unfortunate, like everything, they serve a purpose and this reminds us to be more in tune with ourselves. By encountering these feelings, we are becoming more aware of the sensations within our body on the physical realm. By being aware of when things in our life feel different, or if we feel different than how we usually do, we know it's time to ignite change, to move that energy, to cleanse and protect it. There is always light to be found amidst the darkness.

Use the following technique to protect your energy at any time of day. It can be performed as often as you like, but know that once created, it has the power to protect you for as long as you desire (an entire lifetime or even more). Again, what we need to remember as always is the intention behind the practice. And most importantly, to tune in to your own vibrational frequency.

This simple meditation is ideal to protect your own energy. Try to practice this visualization daily. The more comfortable you become with it, the quicker you will be able to ignite the protection around you.

Energy Protection Meditation

1. Close your eyes and take five deep breaths in and out.

2. Imagine drawing a circle of light energy around your whole body to create a bubble. This bubble of light reaches high above your head and below your feet. This bubble is your sacred space.

3. Recite the following intention: "I command my sacred space."

4. Imagine the light bubble around you as a protective barrier. No harm can enter this sacred space. This energy that circulates around you is beautiful. It's glowing with warmth and magnificent magic. It is calming and replenishing. You are safe, loved, and cared for. Spend your time defining this circle of light.

5. Say the intention again: "This is my sacred space. I am protected always. I am constantly looked after. Only loving energy is welcome in my sacred space."

6. For an even stronger protection, imagine this bubble as a mirrored object and allow the energy of others to be reflected back into themselves, as your own energy remains within.

7. Take it one step further and cleanse your energy within this bubble. Envision a lightning bolt of pure, loving light energy piercing through from the Universe above and erupting in your sacred bubble. It is blasting out any negative vibrations, and only enriching your space, your aura with beautiful, healing, loving light. Welcome that light in.

Recharging Your Energy

Now that you've learned how to cleanse and protect your energy, we need to replace that energy by inviting in high vibrational frequencies. When our energy is recharged, refueled, and nurtured, we are able to achieve whatever goal we desire. We can give our energy lavishly, without feeling needy or depleted, because we are radiating in an abundance of pure, loving light energy.

When our energy is recharged and replenished we are living in a higher vibrational frequency and in this space we are closer to bringing our soul into alignment with our Higher Self.

We harness positive energy through various creative experiments, by connecting with the vibrations of nature, and also when we share life experiences with other energies that are alive, such as people, animals, and food.

Before any spiritual practice, start with stillness in your mind as you connect with your soul. Get a journal that you can use purely for you own personal development, self-reflect your life lessons and document the experiences in your life that bring you joy.

Start by asking yourself:
What makes me happy?
What activities bring me joy?
What environment do I feel good in?
What kind of people do I love being around?
This is the first step in learning how to recharge your energy, by doing the things that you love!

There are many techniques we can use to raise our vibrational frequency, and nurture our soul. As you move through the following suggested list, I invite you to find your own practice that brings forth the greatest feeling of being replenished and nurtured. We are all uniquely different, which is what makes us so beautiful, and therefore we will find that we connect with some exercises more so than others.

Some examples of my favorite ways to recharge your energy are as follows:

1. Meditate and Visualize White Light (Aether Energy)
Visualizations during meditations are extremely potent, and have the ability to cleanse, recharge, and realign your energy. We have the ability to create change in our life with just our thoughts and visualizations. To do so, imagine being completely submersed in white light and that this light is cleansing all negativity and completely filling your energy field up with positive vibrations. Imagine specifically what this energy feels like. Feel the abundance of love that surrounds you as it rejuvenates your aura.

2. Get Into Nature (Earth Energy)
Take time to yourself to reconnect with the Earth anywhere you find natural life. It could be a park, rainforest, beach, mountain or garden. Anywhere that allows space for you to be present with the Earth Energy. Walk around the space tuning into the vibrational frequencies that surrounds you. Be still in this presence and allow the vibrations to nurture your energy as you honor its Spirit Energy.

3. Swimming / Soaking in a Bath (Water Energy)
Water provides an opportunity for rebirth. If you are able to swim amongst the natural salt water of the Earth's crust you will benefit greatly, and if not, do not worry, as there are ways to make your bath

heavenly with essential oils and natural salts. Allow yourself to soak in the water, surrendering any unease within your body and mind; let the Water Energy cleanse and replenish your emotional vibrations.

4. Creative Work (Aether + Earth Energy)

Creative work such as drawing, painting, gardening, cooking, or any activity that uses our hands is able to nurture our soul. This is because when we are working creatively, we are tapping into unconscious energy, we are letting our soul dance through our body with free reign, allowing the love for what we do to take over. When we stop placing limitations on ourselves we are able to let our soul move freely, therefore nurturing our consciousness organically.

5. Sound Energy (Air + Aether Energy)

Aside from listening and dancing to music, singing and playing an instrument also releases energy and invites in harmonious vibrations. Music is a sacred dance between our outer and inner worlds, and when we are truly in the flow of creating harmonic vibrations, whether through our voice or an instrument, we are able to raise our energy field up to new heights which is unable to be achieved in the physical world. Music is truly a gift for our soul to rejoice on Earth.

6. Eating Healthy Vegan Food (Earth Energy)

Feeding our body may sound like an obvious idea, but the question of what you choose to feed your body is one of the greatest choices you hold. Do you feed your soul with heart-nurturing foods that support the natural process of your organs and muscles to repair itself naturally? Or do you eat to support your emotions? Eating a well-balanced, nutritious plant-based diet will provide your body with the support it needs to harmonize the flow of energy between your mind and body, thus enabling you to make confident choices and decisions.

7. Absorbing Sunlight (Fire Energy)

Sun energy provides us with vitamin D, which is crucial to our body's survival on Earth. Sunlight supports our mood (mental health), improves our sleep, as well as boosting our immunity. The energy from the sun provides the entire Earth with life; without it, we cannot survive, and so it's important to make sure you get your daily dose of sunlight, even if it's just for 10 minutes! Close your eyes and stand or lie down in the natural sunlight, allowing the rays to nurture you with love. Be cautious about spending too much time beneath the sun, as with extreme heat, it can cause damage to our skin. There's many natural products you can use to protect your skin whilst still absorbing the nurturing love of sunshine. Be sure to know your limits of what works for you, for even sitting in the shade whilst the energy of the sunlight is present can also be very rewarding.

The importance of all the techniques above lie in your ability to be present in the conscious world, without interruptions, and to allow Source Energy to move from the unconscious realms into your aura.

When you connect with the power of Source Energy you are able to completely release anything that is holding you back from being true to yourself, while replenishing your energy with the love and light from your Higher Self. Think about this as you partake in your exercises. Remember to always set your intention, invite in the energy, visualize its bountiful gifts, and be present as you focus solely on that moment of time to ensure the most rewarding results.

Listen to thy Soul

Although you may search outside
for answers, you will always be brought back into yourself.
Your soul is the only one who knows the pathway of your destiny,
the only one who knows how to honor your heart
to enable the true healing of yourself.

Soul + Spirituality

By now we have established that we have a soul, for we know that there is something greater than us steering our life on this Earth. We know that our soul is made up of energy and that this energy is vibrating constantly. The energy of our soul is everywhere and yet nowhere, all at once (for we cannot define the Universe). Our soul resides in the cosmos, as our Higher Self, and also lives through our bodies to experience this life, as our Spiritual Self. We have a Soul Contract and this is how our destiny plays out, yet we have control over our destiny and therefore we can influence our destiny too. How do we do this though? By learning how to honor, heal and most importantly, listen to our soul.

Every experience in our life has the ability to change our perception of the world and our own understanding of ourselves. Once we have mastered one life lesson, our Soul Contract will throw us a new challenge that will encourage us to raise our vibration up to a higher standpoint to see the world in a new light. In this section we are going to explore how to listen to and love our soul so that we may navigate our Soul Contract and live a truly meaningful life.

We have established that our soul has chosen our body and our life in order to achieve personal fulfillment, or to ascend to the next plane of existence. The idea of having a soul resonates loudly within us because we know from our own experience that there is more to life than just our mind and our body. We can feel that there is something bigger than our own comprehension that is steering the pathway of our life and every so often we will see glimpses of this divine beauty within us. It comes in many forms, perhaps through a voice of reason in our heart that tells us definite answers when there is no sense behind it. Or sometimes we experience surreal coincidences when we visit a place with an uncanny knowing that we have been there before (a memory from a past life). Or at other times we can remember explicit detail of a conversation that we've never had.

Like the Darwin theory of evolution, that our cells and genes adapt according to our environment, we also inherit wisdom that is passed on from previous generations to enable a skillful survival. This adaptation of survival is not limited to physical and mental, for it also carries over the wisdom from our previous lives, and our bloodline, that when harnessed, has the ability to raise our consciousness and remind us of who we really are. Energy never dies, so this ancestral wisdom is evolving as the generations evolve too, but the problem lies amidst the governments and moneymaking corporations today whose main goal is to distract our minds from journeying within to connect with our soul to hear this sage advice.

We are constantly encouraged to participate within the rat race of a nine-to-five daily working schedule in order to make enough money to provide for ourselves and our family. Yet, our true survival comes down to how we look after our soul and the souls of our loved ones around us. If we take the time to connect with our soul, we are able to tap into the infinite wisdom of the cosmos that vibrates within and around our Higher Self. This wisdom has the ability to reveal the truth that will heal the world and all its trauma.

We are living in an incredible time of technological advances and innovative designs, but the focus is not on making a better future for the people or the planet, the focus is on greed and monetary gain. And this is the basis of collective consciousness trauma. We have lost our own identity by ignoring how to connect with ourselves. We think we know how to connect with others through technology but this is a fabricated idea created by the IT designers who encourage people to show only one side of their personality. We need real-life experiences with people and our environment, we need to feel real vibrations of energy. This is where we start our healing journey. The more we learn how to nurture our soul, live authentically with each other, and honor the Earth, the more alive we will feel, thus deepening our life experience. Once we have mastered a connection with ourselves, we will be able to fulfill our own unique life purpose.

If we look to the core matter of our bodies we realize that we are energy floating through space. As we move through this space of existence we perceive our reality around us according to our level of awareness, which is influenced by our beliefs, experiences, and attitudes. As we move through life our perception changes in response to our environment, and depending on the life lessons we have chosen, will determine our awakening process. But still, we need to open ourselves up to the possibility of change, we need to understand that when we lean into challenges with curiosity we are able to change our perception of our world, thus enabling the energy of our soul to transform into higher frequencies. The possibility of being able to climb the spiral ladder of awareness is available to us at any given moment. The invitation to rise will always be possible and ultimately it is our choice as to which vibrational field we wish to live in. As we venture through our life and heal from the difficult challenges and scenarios, we ascend to the next plane and move into a higher level of awareness, one that holds new depths of wisdom and understanding that we could never have imagined before. But this perception of life that we tap into has always existed, it's just that we have moved out of our current vibrational frequency into a new level and therefore, this all feels completely new. And gradually, with each difficulty, and each challenge that we face, our mind breaks open into another viewpoint and we slowly tick off the life lessons of our Soul Contract.

But at no point is our journey of self-discovery ever complete. Throughout our entire life we will deal with life lessons and experiences to challenge us and open ourselves to different perspectives. This isn't to provide discomfort, for as time continues, each outlook gets clearer. They are all serving one purpose: to bring ourselves into alignment with our soul, our Higher Self (us in the purest form). At the heart of each level of ascension we can find the same goal—to bring our awareness into the present moment and to share the love that surrounds us with each other.

So, then what is life? Is it but a dream of holographic visions pieced together from our own vibrational experiences? This is a question with no definite answer, but we need to find safety in the unknown and realize that we have the power to create the answers and definitions ourselves. We can do this by feeling our way into the truth. As our soul floats through this energy field we experience emotions, decipher visions and reveal deeper truths about ourselves.

A personal story about conscious awareness and the power of our mind:
I remember being a child of eight years old sitting outside of school waiting for my mother to pick me up. But on that particular day there was an unexpected cold wind and I had nothing to keep me warm. My whole body was shivering. There was no shelter (being Queensland in Australia, we rarely have cold days), so I was trying to figure out how to keep warm. I stated the question to myself and asked, and the response was to imagine what it felt like to be warm. I closed my eyes and envisioned a fire within me, warming up my whole body. I kept saying to myself, remember how it feels to be warmed up by a fire. And the moment I imagined that fire and how it felt,

I wasn't cold anymore. I opened my eyes quickly, confused as to what had happened, for the warmth within me felt surreal, like I had jumped to another portal. When I opened my eyes I was hit by a ghastly wind, freezing cold, and when I closed my eyes, I could see that fire within me, feeling warm and nurtured. At that moment, at age eight, I realized, that our reality was not as it seemed. And the idea that I had the power to manipulate my reality stayed with me for my whole life. I knew in that moment that our thoughts were beyond powerful and that our reality as we know it, is not what it is. And this is probably one of my most early memories that encouraged me to question "what is reality?"

Our soul, as itself, is pure love. The feelings of emotions, of failures, of success, of happiness and sadness do not belong to it, nor does it actually create these vibrations. These feelings are created in the body and the mind. The moment our soul enters our body as our Spiritual Self in this reality it is as though we have forgotten who we really are (an abundance of love), and each experience, each moment of clarity, and each life lesson brings us one step closer to revealing the truth that we are the creator of our world.

There is so much more to our lives, to ourselves, and the Universe that we cannot possibly understand. Although we may not know how or why we are here, one thing is clear:

The more we honor and connect with our soul, the better we feel, the more clarity we have, and the easier life becomes. Through regular practice of harmonizing our mind, body, and soul, we create balance and peace in our life. When we learn how to honor our soul, we bring forth our desires, passions, and love for life into the light. This provides meaning to our lives.

Your Intuition

Your intuition is the voice of judgement that comes from infinite love.

If we are successful in nurturing our soul and praising our soul we in turn receive infinite wisdom through our intuition—the way in which our Higher Self communicates with us. Our intuition is able to guide us along our life journey to help fulfill our Soul Contract, thus creating internal happiness.

Our role is to clear the mind, look after our body, and nurture our soul to enable a harmonic balance. Our soul likes the challenge, it creates experience, this is our ultimate aim—to feel and experience a wonderful life with great depth and meaning.

So, if our soul knows what we need to do to achieve in this life, if our soul knows the right lessons, we just need to allow ourselves to let it speak. When we establish a connection with our soul we are able to heed the guidance as we embark upon our life journey. The more in tune we are with this side of ourselves, the easier our life becomes. When we master how to communicate with our soul we are able to move past the mind's constant chatter, to enter the sacred space of our soul's vibration and heed any wisdom that we wish. Our soul is always connected to every soul, every spirit, every life force that exists in the Universe at all times. You have the power to tap into the collective unconsciousness and harness this information at any point. But to truly feel this knowledge you need to sharpen a very important spiritual tool, and that is your intuition.

Our intuition is the communication channel between our Spiritual Self (our soul in our human body) and our Higher Self (our soul in the unseen worlds). Our soul can move between these two worlds, the seen and unseen worlds, between our Spiritual Self and our Higher Self, at any moment. Your soul is always residing in both of these two places simultaneously, but when your soul transmutes from the unconscious into consciousness, we forget this truth. And we spend a lot of our life path finding our way back "home." However, there is a way that we can bring forth the wisdom of our Higher Self into consciousness, and this is through our intuition.

How to Connect to Your Intuition

1. Get into a comfortable position and close your eyes.

2. Relax in a meditative state and envision what your Higher Self might look like. It could be a light being of pure bright energy, or perhaps another version of yourself, the ultimate you. Whatever you see, trust it and know that the version of what you see of your Higher Self can change over your life. Because your Higher Self cannot be defined, this is just a projection of what you envision for this particular time of your life. The important element is the energy you feel when being close to your Higher Self. That feeling may grow with time, and the more you learn to vibrate at that same frequency the closer you will become to your Higher Self.

3. Now that you have a strong visual of your Higher Self, imagine a cord of energy that connects you together. This energy cord can be any color and it can connect you from anywhere. Perhaps from your heart, your third eye (which is a chakra energy portal located on your forehead) or your aura. Wherever feels right, just trust it.

4. Examine this energy cord between yourself and your intuition. What does it look like? Is it thick or thin? Is it transparent or spotty? Use your intention to create it how you want it to be. Make it strong with beautiful fluidity. Move through and clear out any blockages or patch up any holes. You have the power to create this communication channel as you wish.

This exercise has established the communication channel between your Spiritual Self and your Higher Self, your intuition. This energy cord allows your soul to move from the unseen realms as your Higher Self through to your body easily, and vice versa. This connection can never be cut. Sometimes it may fall weak, and other times it may be thick and strong, but it will never diminish. This is your communication channel and the pathway of your intuition. There are many ways to strengthen this communication channel and there are different ways that will enable you to hear the voice of your soul. As we mentioned before with the difference between religion and spirituality, we hear the voice of our intuition and our soul speaking through to us in spirituality, whereas in religion, that voice that devotees would be hearing would be who they refer to as God. But in spirituality, a strong belief is that you are your own God.

Now that you have established what your intuition channel could look like, let's look at some spiritual tools to help strengthen your intuition.

Meditation

Meditation is a family of techniques that retrains the focus of your attention. The more we meditate, the louder the voice of our intuition speaks. This is because we are bringing our awareness into a stage of non-attachment and non-resistance. When we meditate, our soul travels from our external body and up into the unseen worlds back into our Higher Self so that it can replenish and rejuvenate its energy. The journey from our reality to our Higher Self can take time to master, but the deeper we lean into meditation, the easier the pathway becomes. Once the pathway has been established, every time you meditate, you strengthen that journey. With consistent practice you will be able to enter a state of pure bliss upon closing your eyes, for you will travel quickly into the space of unconsciousness, realigning with your Higher Self, learning the knowledge and wisdom that you aspire to attain. The more time you spend connecting with your Higher Self, the easier it becomes to dance between these two worlds —the seen and unseen—and when you have mastered this technique it will become a natural process for you to bring forth the knowledge and wisdom from the unseen into your consciousness. From this space you will be able to view your life with complete clarity, removing your layers of perception to be able to see things clearly as they really are.

This concept of what meditation brings is not a theory, there have been countless scientific studies proving the benefits of meditation. These studies conclude that continuous meditation creates a positive impact on mental health. Meditation has shown to reduce stress, control anxiety, ease depression, enhance self-awareness, improve your sleep, and increase your focus, to name a few. And it makes sense! If meditation is able to retrain your focus, you are able to let go of the thoughts that are detrimental to your wellbeing, and focus your energy on to the thoughts that raise your vibration higher, and thoughts that inspire you to become the greatest version of yourself. The more comfortable you become with meditation, the easier it is to travel into the unseen worlds to your Higher Self and the stronger the voice of your intuition grows, enabling your true self to be present as you live your greatest life.

Think of your mind as though it is a wheel on a bike, and you're riding your way through life. Sometimes the road is hard, rocky, and muddy, and other times (our favorite times), it's smooth and carefree. Like any wheel, after some time, the sides fill up with mud and dirt, and get clogged. The edges might get rusty. So to keep the wheel in the best shape possible, we need to spend time cleansing and revitalizing the wheel for new pathways, to allow fluid motions. If we take care of cleaning our wheel regularly we can handle any kind of road that comes our way. Any pathway that opens itself up to us, we can handle, because we have grown strength from our previous journey and are ready to take on new challenges. This is what meditation does: it clears your mind of anything that is detrimental to your emotional wellbeing. The more you practice clearing your mind, the easier your life path will become.

There are many forms of meditation around the world. I am sharing with you the core basics for anyone to get started. When I personally create meditations, I like to start with this, and then explore a creative visualization journey with music. When meditating on my own, I sit in silence and allow my soul to journey as it pleases.

How to Meditate

1. Close your eyes and get into a comfortable position, either sitting up with your back supported or lying down.

2. Bring your attention to your breath and breathe in and out very slowly for at least five breaths. This will calm your mind and body down to a state of complete peace.

3. Become the observer and allow your thoughts to float by with no judgement. As any thoughts arise, let them arise, acknowledge them, but then let them go. If at any point you find yourself drifting (being carried along with your thoughts), bring your attention back to your breath and calm yourself once more. Your breath is a way to anchor your attention on the present moment. So come back to it as often as you need.

This is the core basics of meditation. Simply closing your eyes, keeping your mind clear, and allowing your breath to guide you. When ready, you may follow through with a body scan as explained in number 4, or a creative visualization as shown in number 5.

4. To scan your body: move your awareness around to different areas of your body and notice any sensations that arise. Start at your feet and work your way up to your head. As you navigate through, use your breath to blow any stagnant energy that is weighing you down, encouraging greater relaxation. This practice turns your attention into a gentle state of unconscious awareness. Be aware that you are meditating, but choose not to define anything (do not bring the unconscious into consciousness).

5. After several minutes (with practice), you may find your imagination begins to explore. You may be presented with colors, symbols, or images which are messages from the unseen worlds, and this is the commencement of a journey through to the realm of unconsciousness. You can guide yourself through this space in your meditation, asking for guidance and specific symbols to be shown. Or, you can be taken on a journey in a guided meditation practice (which is my favorite form of meditation to record!).

Creative visualization and imagination does not always occur to everyone, and those who experience it are in no way superior, nor is it the goal. Trust that whatever you see or experience is what is meant for you. And take note of how your meditation practice evolves over time.

If you are new to meditation start with either guided meditations, or practice this process for 5 - 10 minutes and gradually work your way up to 20 minutes to 1 hour for best results each day. Some people believe that the rewards are greater when you meditate at the same time every day, and also when trying to do it twice a day. Find what program works for you. The more consistent you are with it, the stronger your results will become.

Journaling

Journaling is a creative outlet that channels your intuition and supports your mental health. When you allow yourself to express your internal thoughts with no judgement or fear, the energy of the emotion is able to be spoken and released through a tangible method. When we turn to journaling to express ourselves we are able to identify the cause of the problem as well as suggest solutions on how to fix it. This provides you with clarity on difficult situations and enables you to view your scenarios from a larger scale (a bird's eye view), thus encouraging self-reflection and self-improvement.

When we look at our problems from afar, (as though in third person), we tap into the advice and knowledge that we so wisely know. This is why we often are better at giving advice to others than applying it to ourselves because we see the situation from afar and aren't emotionally involved and so from this space, everything is clear. We need to use the same idea of getting out of our head space and seeing the situation we are encountering as though we are not personally involved. This enables us to see the truth and transparency for what it really is, thus analyzing our thoughts in a cohesive order. As we explore our emotions and feelings around a subject we can release the energy from our mind, allowing new vibrations to take its place.

Journaling can also be seen as a form of therapeutic meditation. Like meditation, the purpose is to clear our thoughts and allow them to be expressed and released. When we express ourselves in our journal we are sharing our story and therefore, we are healing. We don't have time to hover over one particular thought; we are constantly writing from pencil to paper, getting in a rhythmic flow of thought cleansing.

Benefits of journaling include mental health support, enhancing problem solving, and improving physical illness by clearing the emotional baggage and mental blocks connected to our problems.

How to Journal

1. Find a blank notebook that you can keep for yourself.

2. Always start your journaling by writing the date as this will assist in your own personal journey of self-reflection and self-awareness.

3. Start by writing down how you feel. You can write it in a stream-of-consciousness type format where the purpose is to just allow the words and feelings to flow. Or you could do it by listing key points as to the emotions that you felt today.

4. As you move through your emotions and feelings, see if there are any situations or memories that arise and write them down. Often we can view situations and scenarios in a different way by writing down the story as to what happened. Sometimes just writing down your thoughts is enough, other times you might want to self-reflect. As you review your current problems, ask yourself:

   What happened today that made me feel uncomfortable?
   How can I turn this negative into a positive?
   How can I learn from this experience for the better?
   How do others perceive my actions?
   Is there a deeper meaning that I need to reveal?
   If a friend was telling me this story, what's the advice I would give them?

The more we connect and reflect how we feel, the clearer the voice of our intuition becomes as we identify what it is that brings us joy or sadness.

There is nothing to fear within your own mind. This is a safe space. This is a sacred time with yourself, a time for you to honor yourself with the respect that you deserve. Because when we sit in silence, pen to paper, and allow the words to flow through us without judgement is when we create magic. We channel a higher entity that voices our inner thoughts and brings to life our emotions into a tangible existence.

You can also use journaling as a spiritual tool to create a direct dialogue through your intuition with your Higher Self. You can channel your Higher Self by writing down a question, and answer it immediately without thinking. This is allowing the voice of your intuition to speak clearly, because your mind has not interfered. Like everything, it takes practice, and this is best done after meditation when your mind has been cleared and your energy is calm.

Another form of journaling that has proven to ignite positive change in people's lives is a "gratitude journal." The way this is done is by documenting morning and/ or evening a list of things you are grateful for. As an alternative or in addition to this, list the things that you are proud of yourself for. The idea behind this is that by listing things we are grateful for it in turn attracts more things to be grateful for. The basis for this principle falls upon the law of attraction, which we will explore more later in this book when we discuss manifesting. It relies on the idea that at the core of our body is vibrating energy (atoms). And it is scientifically proven that like energy attracts like energy. Therefore, as we list things we are grateful for, we relive the feeling that they emit, hence bringing our vibrations into a higher frequency. As we continue to live in this higher vibrational field, we in turn attract more like energy, thus bringing forth more things in our lives to be grateful for.

Our intuition is an energy channel, and like the energy of our soul, we are learning how to nurture this energy channel. Practice different tools and techniques and be aware of what is working for you. Keep these ideas in your journal and incorporate them into your daily rituals to continue strengthening your communication channel with your soul.

Understanding Emotional Wellbeing

Mental health can be described as a dissociation between our soul and our reality. To understand this, think of it as though your soul is floating above your body and cannot land in reality. In depression, we feel as though we are having an out-of-body experience as our negative emotions are amplified in extreme and we cannot understand them, we cannot connect to them, and most often, we feel numb. With anxiety, again, our soul is out of our body, but this time our mind is taking over, hurrying along and pushing our body to move in strange ways. In both cases, we need to learn to bring ourselves into the present moment, practice grounding our soul into our body, becoming connected to reality, and from here we build the strength to remind ourselves of the power we hold to control our life.

Becoming aware of our emotional wellbeing is essentially becoming aware of what it is that makes our soul truly happy. What are you doing that brings joy to your soul? And what are you doing that causes your soul pain? Have a look at your daily habits and find where in your life you can create change to bring forth nurturing love and praise to your soul.

So often we want, and are conditioned to want, a quick fix to make everything better. We are happy to take a prescription drug if it means we don't have to deal with the problem, but we are unaware that our temporary fix of the problem creates an entirely new issue. We take a pill that numbs our emotions even further, pushing us farther away from our true connection with our soul, thus ignoring the core problem that requires deep change within our life. We in turn find ourselves feeling better and we have replaced the absence of feeling depressed or anxious to feeling dependent on an outside force to provide us with the inner peace that we seek. Those who are reliant on these forms of drugs become completely dissociated with who they really are, and quickly the spiral is created of attachment issues, intimacy problems, and difficulty to live a happy life. Sadly, this kind of lifestyle of ignoring the problem has become normal in many countries around the world. We need to speak up and share our story with others and learn from one another so that we can help each other heal. Diet, our environment, and spiritual philosophy all play a key role in our healing process. And when we share our story with others we learn what worked for them and it inspires us to find solutions ourselves.

At some point in our lives we are all confronted with a battle against our mind; we feel like we are drowning in our emotions, and we are searching for something to bring more meaning and depth to our life. If we share our story with others we won't feel so alone; we will realize that what we feel happens to everyone, and we will learn different ways to cope, to self-soothe, and to get that strength back within us. Remind yourself that these emotions of sadness, fear, and sorrow will not last; like all energy they will move through and transform, but the trick is for you to learn how to nurture that energy when it arises, how to allow your body to become the alchemist to transform energy. It's important that we acknowledge and recognize our pain yet step out of the victimizing persona, by realizing that we have the power within to make the changes that we seek.

The first technique to help self-soothe is grounding (as we explored on page 54). Grounding (also called Earthing) is the process of grounding your soul back into your body and claiming your space here on Earth. By connecting with Earth Energy you are connecting to Source Energy and reminding your soul where you are, and most importantly who you are. Who are you?

You are an angelic being of pure, loving light energy having a conscious experience on Earth.

The easiest way to ground myself is to walk outside and feel the Earth beneath my feet. If it's not available, I like to burn some white sage, cleanse the air, and purify my mind. I meditate often, although it helps (doing this regularly), I find I need something more to pull me out of the drag. And I resort to oils and smells. Perhaps it's a way of keeping things fresh. The main thing is to push myself to go outside and walk in the fresh air. Even though it might be freezing and maybe I have nowhere to go. Just getting outside and remembering how big the world is and how tiny and little I am in comparison reminds me that there are answers nearby. I think of life like a river flowing. And the water just organically flows effortlessly down the stream. Just flowing beautifully. But one day, you get stuck behind a rock in the stream. And the water usually splits and moves either side, but you can't. You are just stuck behind this rock. Stuck, in this locked time frame. Unable to move. That's what depression feels like. Unable to move forward. Accept that you are in this place, surrender to whatever may come and open yourself up to change, to help move alongside the flowing rivers of life.

Mental health consists of multiple layers and there is rarely a quick fix. We need to work on ourselves to get to the core of the problem, to understand what our soul needs that we aren't providing. We can do this by trying new routines and different activities every day and by taking note of how we feel before and afterwards. Diet and our environment also play a key role in our mental health, for our emotions can also change due to deficiencies in nutrients and vitamins. As you journey through to learn how to support your emotional wellbeing, know that by having an open mind and experimenting is the pathway to healing yourself. But before doing this, it's important to understand and acknowledge your own emotions and feelings with anxiety or depression so that you can recognize the signs for preventative measures later down your life path. The more you practice harmonizing the flow of energy between your mind, body, and soul through self-care practices, the less likely depression and anxiety will have a chance to overcome your rationality.

Mental health issues happen to everyone so don't be scared to ask for help. You are never alone in feeling this way, and although what you are going through feels unique to you, it helps to talk to others, to share stories and learn each other's self-soothing technique. Because we all have at least one, even if we don't realize it!

The more familiar you become with your own changes of emotions, the easier it will be to identify what influences those feelings and what area of your life needs attention. It's important to not only understand how you are feeling, but potentially to learn why you are feeling this way. I'll give you an example.

A personal story about my own journey through depression:

When I lived in northern Europe I was very depressed. To the point, I felt numb, I felt like a zombie, switching between oversleeping and insomnia. Unable to focus, or bring meaning to my life. I felt claustrophobic, as though a heavy entity was pushing down on me, sucking the light and laughter from my soul. I allowed myself to bask in the darkness for a little while, but days turned into weeks, and even months. And before I knew it, I forgot what it was like to be me. The real me. I was in a state of non-acceptance to the present moment and it felt impossible to find my way back home. When I searched within to ask why, my intuition told me that it was the change of weather (we had just entered winter), and the lack of sunlight was extremely abrupt to my natural cycle. But I was stuck; I was unable to travel to a place with sunshine, and instead had to learn how to soothe myself in other ways. I did this through nurturing my energy with what was available around me.

I grounded my soul with Earth Energy, although it was freezing to get out into nature, I forced myself to. I nurtured my soul with Water Energy by taking warm baths and giving love back to myself. I harnessed Fire Energy with the warmth of indoor fireplaces at any chance I could. And even though it was cold, I breathed in fresh clean Air Energy everyday. I fed my mind with wisdom and used this down time to explore the darkness that I was feeling. I knew it wasn't going to last and so I made friends with it. I had experienced depression before, and so I knew that it wasn't going to stay. And instead, I opened myself to see if there was a lesson to be learned. I opened my mind to believe there was greater meaning for me. And only after I exited this pain, only after I felt myself again, I could see the reasons why, and a big part of that was to find ways to self-soothe and create happiness in my life even though I felt nothing inside. During this time of solitude was when I wrote my Daily Rituals *book as these were my affirmations and exercises that kept me going, and I also created my first poetry book,* Define Me Divine Me. *If you have this poetry book, you will read very dark explorations of my journal entries, but like all darkness, light exists; you just need to be willing to find it. The only positive I found from sitting in this darkness was that I was able to channel incredible beauty and wisdom. I believe some of my greatest writing occurs in this darkness, for I am seeking so hard to find the light within, and writing through it is my only way out.*

The word darkness may trigger a sharp emotion within us. Some of us feel fear, others feel pain. Either way, we need to become friends with it and know that there is nothing to be feared. If we resist what is, we will become stagnant, and pause our growth. We need to evolve and grow through the experience, understand that we are transitioning into another version of ourselves. To assist this progression of our transitioning stage it helps to analyze our life thoroughly, asking the soul-searching questions of "who am I?" and "what do I need?" to find out where in our life we aren't giving ourselves what it is that our soul craves. What more could you be doing to ignite change, to allow the energy to transmute through you?

When we are faced with mental health challenges, we need to understand that we are having disturbances in our flow of energy between the mind, body, and soul. This energy that circulates in a continuous cycle is out of balance and the secret is to find what in your life you can change in order to stabilize the flow of energy once more. Your energy wants to be moving freely and transforming and expanding. It's only if we choose to stop that from happening will we find ourselves in agony. When we entertain thoughts that provide us with no benefit or hold on to past memories that cause us pain, we are literally holding on to stagnant energy and that energy is unable to flow through us to transform.

When we look at our anxiety or depression as trapped energy, as energy that does not belong within us, it becomes easier to learn how to move it through us. We need to remember that we are an alchemist of energy; we need to remind ourselves to transform the negative energy within us into the blessing that it has the potential to be.

Healing Our Wellbeing

The moment you begin to notice the darkness taking charge inside you, sit with it and listen, for it has a lot to teach you. Find a quiet place where you feel safe on your own. This could be in your bedroom or perhaps amongst nature. Scan through your energy field to find out what is going on within. Witness your emotions and observe them without judgement or resistance. Accept that they exist and remind yourself that they do not define you.

This darkness is a calling from within your soul to let you know that something is not right. That something in your world needs to be changed. The journey is to find out what that something is. Perhaps your boundaries have been crossed. Maybe you are filling your days with activities that don't nurture your soul. Maybe you are in the wrong relationship, the wrong environment of what it is that your soul thrives. Sit with a journal and write through the surplus or lack of feelings.

First, define your emotions by asking yourself questions such as:
How am I feeling?
Where in my body is this darkness / trapped energy?
If this trapped energy was a color, what color would it be?
Is this color clear and fluid? Thick, thin, muggy?
What's the texture? How large is it?
Where did this emotional color come from?
What has happened to make me feel this way?
What changes can I make in my life to help me heal this pain within?
How can I soothe this energy, or change my emotional state?

After you have identified the texture, color, and density of the energy you need to heal, look at the techniques from the previous section on Universal Energies where we explore cleansing and replenishing your energy field (page 65). When we describe the energy, we are bringing the unconscious into our consciousness, and in this space, we can focus our attention on clearing it out of our aura. Once this is done, you will have a closer insight to determine the root of the problem. And from here, we can journal and meditate to let our soul speak to us and tell us what it needs. You can set this up in a ritual space (page 115), meditate, and then write down the following questions. Write your responses immediately without thinking, or speak the question and let the first answer be presented before you.

Why am I unhappy?

What area of my life do I need to change?

What am I denying myself of?

What should I be doing to support my future self?

What do I need to let go of?

What do I need to invite in?

How can I make this change?

Reflect over your answers and propose a solution for each response. This solution may not work, or it might be exactly what you need. The point is to experiment! And even if it isn't exactly what you need, have faith that it will lead you to the solution that will work. Your soul needs change, so by trying different things out you are creating that change for yourself.

Darkness in our life is necessary to our personal development, for without darkness we cannot define light. Both are needed to create wholeness; they are together under the same umbrella. So until we learn to embrace both the darkness and light within us, we will be stagnant in our growth. For our growth is dependent on learning how to navigate the darkness within us. Such moments of terror may spark questions within that change our perception of life forever. In these grim moments we are able to see true beauty around us. But it's up to you to want to see this magic; it's your choice to choose to align with love instead of fear. If you believe that you will never get better, then you will stay in a victimizing state until you change your mind. If you are ready to find the answers, be still, observe the changes within you, accept them, and be open to whatever comes your way. Entering the darkness does not require strength; it does not require us to become dark either. It requires the simple observation of what is stirring within you, accepting that it exists, while you allow the energy to move through you.

The more comfortable you become with your emotional state, the easier it will be listen to your intuition as to what is going on inside of you. We need to ask the question of "what is it here to teach me?" Check in with yourself and see if you are living in the present moment and if you are grounded in your body (page 54).

Understanding depression is difficult. Most of the time we don't really know that we are experiencing it, and even when we do, the hardest part is telling our loved ones to be patient with us, and trying to ask them to understand even though you are trying to understand yourself. Remind yourself that this feeling is only temporary, that it does not define you and find the spiritual tools that help you transition through this energy.

Here are eight steps to encourage the energy to move through and to help get you into a more positive routine when faced with depression.

Eight Steps for Depression

1. Get out of bed and have a shower or bath

Hygiene is always important and especially when you don't feel very good. Water cleanses our skin and replenishes the energy of our soul. Bring your mind into the present moment as you connect with water and allow its energy to wash away your thoughts and low vibrational feelings, as you open yourself up to new possibilities. As the water washes over your body and head, visualize the pure lightness of energy clearing away any darkness within you. Encourage Water Energy to cleanse your aura with the visualization process found on page 58. This is a great way to begin your day whenever you feel depressed.

2. Get dressed in happy clothes

It may sound silly, but dressing in your favorite clothes that make you feel good is important too. Even if you want to lounge in sweatpants all day, that's fine—but choose your favorite sweatpants! Wear your most comfiest tee, your most nurturing snuggly socks. Choose clothes that make you happy and feel good.

3. Meditation always helps depression

Even if it's only for 10 minutes, at least that little bit of meditation will help you get out your headset and make a difference to bring a sense of peace to your mind. If your mind is too busy it helps to listen to guided meditations. Depression is the reason I began meditating, and I was so impressed with the results that I became a meditation teacher to help others.

4. Go for a walk

Walking outside helps bring a change of perspective to your mind and is a great energy boost to help deal with depression. By interacting outside of your usual space you remind yourself that there is something else out there. Something bigger than yourself. Even if it's just a walk around the block, look at the wonders of life buzzing around you. Take a moment to look deeply at the trees, the ground, the sun, the plants, and breathe in the fresh air.

5. Find a creative outlet

Choose something that gets you active and busy reconnecting with the unlimited creative source within your soul. For me personally, I enjoy writing, but I also like to draw, paint, and color-in. Sometimes cooking helps, or gardening. Anything to do with your hands where you don't have to think too much and you can just focus on creating something wonderful is all you need! Bring your mind to the present moment and let your soul play.

6. Write a list of five things you are proud of

This can be anything you have accomplished in your life, or perhaps just in the last day. For example, "I am proud of myself for getting out of bed. I'm proud of myself for smiling in the mirror."

7. Write a list of five things you are grateful for

This can be anything at all! For example, "I am grateful for clean water to drink. I am grateful I get to spend the day resting and nurturing my mind." The more things we give gratitude for, the more things we will receive gratitude for.

8. Acceptance of Self

What you are going through will pass, but for this moment in time it's important to accept that this is happening. Try to find peace in your current situation; say to yourself, "It's okay to feel this way, this feeling will pass."

Take this list and add to it; amend it to make it yours. What you want are activities that create positive acceptance of who you are, and an openness to heal so that you may transform into who it is that you need to become.

Anxiety is another experience that is completely different for everyone. Some feel their heart beating faster, their breath becoming shorter, or their body shaking. Others cannot let go of worry, panic, or of negative thoughts, and these thoughts can begin to take over their rationality. Whatever the symptom, the problem is the same—your body and mind are functioning too rapidly for you to redeem control. But you do have control, you just need to remind yourself and focus your attention on what you can control. Anxious feelings are the result of stress in your body and mind in regards to your current lifestyle.

What can you change in your environment today to support your future self?

When dealing with anxiety it's important to know your own symptoms so that you have an automatic self-soothing technique if anxiety is triggered within you. These techniques vary from person to person, but before any kind of technique can be done, we need to focus on our breath to anchor our soul and calm our mind.

5-4-3-2-1 Anxiety Technique for Grounding

This technique is a very common coping mechanism taught to therapists around the world, because it works! After calming your breath and breathing slowly, look around and acknowledge the following:

5 x things you can see (and look at them) i.e. a cup, pen, window
4 x things you can touch (and touch them) i.e. your hands, a book
3 x things you can hear (and listen) i.e. car sounds, noises of the fridge
2 x things you can smell (and smell them) i.e. coffee beans, flowers
1 x thing you can taste (and taste them) i.e. water, your own teeth

Meditation and journaling are useful tools to help prevent depression and anxiety. The reason they work well for mental health, aside from the clarity and distance of negative thoughts, is because we dissolve the illusion that we have no control over our lives. Through self-reflection we can understand where we are lacking love for ourselves, we can identify where the off-balance in our lives resides, and how we can change this. Once we learn what is needed, it's our responsibility to make these changes in our life. When we focus our attention on empowering ourselves we feel more confident to gain back that control over our life.

We heal our anxiety the same way we heal depression, in that we need to search for the root of the problem and find what it is that needs to be changed in our life. But often, with anxiety, we are attached to a fear or a negative thought that something is going to hurt us and ruin our life. We have convinced ourselves with the belief that something won't change. When we are anxious we are living with worries, fears, and stress about what could happen; we are living in a false reality. You have the power to create the life that you want. If your life isn't aligned with the cravings of your soul then you will be told through these anxious feelings and you will need to change it. Often, we have limitations that forbid us to make drastic changes, but by being aware of what you do want, and making a very small step toward that goal, will make a huge difference to your mental health. We need to envision hope and remind ourselves that we are worthy of achieving our dreams. We need to find purpose in our life and encourage ourselves to consistently practice calling that purpose into our life daily.

To calm yourself in anxiety, you need to ground yourself and bring your awareness into the present moment. The more "present" you become, the less you will be living in fear or holding on to these negative thoughts. There is no space in the present moment for these fears and limiting beliefs. So the more you align with your Higher Self, the more present you become. Being present can feel like meditating with your eyes open. You are observing your life with no judgement, no thoughts or definitions, simply just by being present and aware. Try this technique to be present:

How to Be Present

1. Find an object in front of you and gaze gently as you breathe with ease. Allow yourself to be the observer and in this space, eliminate any thoughts that may enter your mind by accepting them and releasing them.

2. If your mind goes to a negative thought, drop it, let it go, and say the word "peace" to remind you and readjust your focus. Use your breath to anchor your awareness before you.

3. Ignite this awareness of presence as you partake in activities such as going for a walk, watering the garden, or folding washing. Find the simple moments of bliss that you can give yourself in unexpected ways.

Just like with meditation, the more we practice being present the more natural it becomes for us to hold this outlook on our life and the more presence we invite into our day.

Positive Affirmations

I hold my head high, aligned with my Higher Self as I surrender
wholeheartedly into the power of the Universe.
I keep my eyes focused, I release any fears
as I open my heart to the magic of the Universe.
I let go of any negative thoughts that creep into my mind,
for I know that my feelings do not define me.
All my emotions are merely visitors, just testing my patience,
my knowledge, trust and faith in the Universe.
I am resilient and strong.
I am capable of achieving my dreams.
There is nothing holding me back from receiving my success,
it's only if I choose to side with fear,
only if I breathe life into the things that do not serve me.
And so, I am aware of my vibration, I check in with my feelings,
I stay aligned with love,
and I side with the beautiful energy of the Universe.
For I am one with the Universe.
I am the creator of my reality.
I am worthy of love.
I am worthy of miracles and success.
I am everything that I want to be.
I am me.

Honor thy Soul

I close my eyes and feel the infinite love that surrounds me.
I know that I am worthy of receiving this love
for I believe in myself and my unique presence in the world.
I have faith that I am always looked after by my Higher Self
for I have all the answers I could ever ask for.
I choose to put my needs first, knowing that from this place
I can give more to others.
I accept myself as I am right in this moment,
as I peacefully surrender any fears or worries
wholeheartedly into the divine love of the Universe.

Sacred Space

Solitude is sacred. When we have time alone with our soul we can reconnect with our Higher Self. It's in this space that we can give love back to ourselves in whatever way we wish to. It's in this space that we can listen to what it is that makes us truly happy and in turn self-reflect over our actions, and create a plan to support the desires of our life. If you want to implement change, this is the time to do it. It's where we build the strength to be the best version of ourselves.

If you ever feel lonely when you are by yourself, this is a drastic calling for self-love. Because you are beautiful, talented, and capable of giving so much love, why do you give it all away? Why not give it to yourself first so that you can give even higher vibrations to others? The more we learn about ourselves, learn what makes us happy and how to nurture and honor our soul, the more pleasurable life will become.

Creating our sacred space is crucial to our happiness. You need stability, security and safety as part of the building blocks for your foundational needs. Without this element, you will feel lost and searching for comfort. Creating your own sacred space doesn't mean you need to have the most fanciest room or luxurious products, it just means that you have an area where you can honor your soul with the praise that you deserve.

To create your sacred space, you want to find the things that you love in your life. If you have your own room, make sure this room is filled with things that make you happy. And if you are unable to have your own space right now, please work toward creating an area just for you. It doesn't need to be big—just a corner, a windowsill, a dressing table, or even a drawer. When you find this space that represents your soul, fill it with the things that bring you joy and decorate it with inspiration. Display any items that make you happy, such as drawings, photos, quotes, books, ornaments, anything that brings you joy, and display these objects in your space.

We also want to create a sacred altar to ignite rituals of your choice. Rituals, although they stem from Witchcraft and Shamanism of Indigenous tribes, have evolved over time to suit the modern world. To create your sacred altar, you need to find something to represent each of the five elements of Universal Energy that we explored earlier throughout this book page 49. Suggestions and details are as follows:

Earth Energy represents grounding, nurturing, stability, and harvesting. Plants are a beautiful representation of Earth Energy to bring into your space. Their energy of life provides you with peace, and draws you back to the source of creation. If you don't have much of a green thumb, house plants that are easy to keep alive are bamboo or succulents and there's also peace lily, and snake plants (but be careful with pets as some plants are toxic for them, yet air purifying for us!). My other favorite representation of Earth Energy are crystals. Not only are they beautiful, but they hold angelic energy of a high vibrational frequency. The power of crystal energy is able to heal your own vibration, it is able to harmonize the flow of energy within the room, as well as be used for a strong tool for divination. When choosing a crystal it is best to go to a local shop or market as the crystal's energy will call out to you. Casually look over the crystals and allow yourself to be drawn to whichever crystal pulls your attention. This is the right crystal for you. After you choose, research as to what that crystal means; I am positive that the meaning will resonate with you. We are always changing and evolving, so whenever you feel like it's time to buy a new crystal, do the same thing. Crystals make beautiful gifts too, and if you feel inclined to give it someone, do so, for the energy of the crystal may be called elsewhere. Cleansing and recharging your crystals are important too. Their vibrations can be cleansed and recharged like ourselves. To cleanse, wash the crystal in salt water (some crystals deteriorate in water, so check first), and/ or smudge the crystal with white sage. To recharge the crystal, bury the crystal in dirt for a few hours, or place it under the moonlight of a full moon. You will know when it's the right time to smudge and cleanse your crystals as you become more connected with them. You can cleanse and recharge your crystals every few days, weeks or months, whatever feels right for you is right for them.

Water Energy represents nurturing our emotions, a reminder to surrender into the flow of life. To represent Water Energy, a simple jar of water, or even a glass of water that you fill up each time works. If you love teas, treat yourself to a special teapot and make a lovely heartwarming tea to sit on your altar with you whilst creating your ritual. Bring the tea into your ritual, set your intention with the tea, and drink the tea after. Seashells or a small bowl of sand are also representative of Water Energy. Be mindful of the ecosystem when collecting seashells as many sea creatures rely on these shells for survival. Ensure that there are no living creatures in the shells that you collect, and never collect spiral shells as many hermit crabs take empty ones to live in as they grow bigger. Even small flat shells can be used by fish to shelter from predators. So when collecting, try to just take one. Everything naturally created is regenerated and recycled, so we need to be cautious of the role we play in this world.

Fire Energy represents transformation; it ignites creativity and sexuality. To represent Fire Energy, I love to use a candle. Be sure to find an eco-friendly candle that burns non-toxic wax, and is in a glass jar or tin. I love lighting a candle to symbolize the beginning of my ritual, and blowing it out at the end. But if a candle is not possible, find something red or perhaps a piece of bark or wood. You can use a red crystal—items can be crossed over for usage too, but it is nice to have separate things to honor each element on their own. If I was to use a red crystal for fire, I would use different colored crystal for Earth, or a plant for Earth, etc.

Air Energy represents lightness of being and clarity in our mind. Elements for Air Energy are incense, essential oils, a feather (be sure to put the feather found on the ground into the freezer to kill off any diseases). When choosing essential oils it can be difficult if you cannot smell them prior, but most of them smell absolutely delicious! For essential oils I will usually look for their benefits first, and then choose them (the opposite way to how I choose crystals). If you can smell them as testers in a shop then by all means try and see which ones you are drawn to. Be cautious with essential oils as some can be overused and are dangerous when swallowed (especially near children). Some of my favorite essential oils and a few of their benefits are below but there are so many more! These are the oils that I have with me at all times.

Rosemary: Relieves pain and strengthens memory
Ylang Ylang: Nurtures mental health, lowers blood pressure
Frankincense: Anti-inflammatory, improves asthma, cancer fighting
Jasmine: Antiseptic, anti-depressant
Peppermint: Supports digestive issues, relief for headache
Teatree: Hand sanitizer, insect repellent, natural antiseptic

Spirit/ Aether Energy represents yourself, and also your spirit guides, ancestors, or any angelic energy that you wish to honor. Choose any totem that represents this energy to you. It may be a figurine, or a stone. It could be nothing that even resembles Aether Energy at all, but it represents spirit to you and that's what is important. Try to find something to represent yourself and another item to represent spirit as a whole. You can also use photographs, an illustration you drew, or some words. Anything tangible that can represent this unconscious matter.

All of the items you choose can be changed as you feel, and you can always add to them whenever you come across items that suit your sacred space. Once you have gathered your items to represent each of the Universal Energies place them on your sacred space in whatever order you wish to. Decorate and make this space beautiful, because the angelic spirits in the unseen realms are also attracted to your unique view of beauty. Now that you have set up your sacred space, in the next section we will explore what kind of rituals you can create to honor your soul.

My Personal Story about Creating My Sacred Space

I was a peculiar child with a vivid imagination who had an obsession with witches, fairies, and magic. I spent my childhood creating stories of these ideas, bringing them forth into my life. And when I played, I would reenact witches' magic, gathering tools from the garden to ignite my own initiation into their world. As I grew up I dismissed my childhood antics as an eclectic imagination, telling my adult self that fairytales couldn't be real. Although I had let go of the magic of fairies, a spiritual connection to the unseen realms had taken over in its place. As I explored my own inner journey through my travels, learning from spiritual leaders around the world, I found that they all had one thing in common—a spiritual space that honored the Universal Energies.

I wanted to recreate that altar at home one day, but when I went home to do so, I didn't have to, for it was already sitting next to my bed! I had been unconsciously creating my sacred altar since a child. Most of my friends kept make-up and jewelry on their dressing table, but mine was filled with unusual objects that I had gathered over the course of my life. My whole table was already vibrating with these energies. But the most strangest part of it all was a small box that I kept in my handbag. It was a tiny case that I had been carrying around with me since I was no more than 10 years old. It was a box that brought me joy, it was my lucky charm, something that I never left home without. And still, 25 years later, it has never changed. I rarely open it, I just always knew that it was filled with my favorite things and it symbolized strength to me.

When I finally opened it up many years later I found:

- *a snake skin (representing transformation/ Aether Energy)*
- *a small crystal stone (Earth Energy)*
- *a feather (Air Energy)*
- *a letter of encouragement (self-love/ Spirit Energy)*
- *a gift from my deceased grandmother (Ancestor energy)*
- *a small shell (Water Energy)*
- *small wooden charm (Fire Energy)*

I had been unconsciously carrying around my own sacred altar since I was a child!

Rituals

Rituals are an important tool to use in your spiritual pathway of personal development. Rituals are spiritual ceremonies from ancient traditions that can be found in every Indigenous tribe around the world from the earliest civilizations. Up until the last few hundred years has the term ritual been used to symbolize a religious connection. But today, we use the idea of ritual to symbolize many activities. What is needed, with all spiritual work, is your intention behind the ritual alongside an action with something sacred (your sacred space). Perhaps every morning you pick out the same piece of jewelry to wear that represents love from another; that is a form of ritual, because you are bringing forth that idea of feeling love into your daily life repeatedly.

Rituals are primarily used as a sacred ceremony for celebrations. They are a beautiful creation to honor the divine energy within us and around us. In our rituals we call upon unconscious energy and invite it to come forth into our consciousness, thus raising our vibrations in unity with our Higher Self.

How to Create Your Own Ritual

Every ritual needs to have three elements: intention, sacred space, and an action.

Intention:
Your intention is your reason for the ritual.
What do you hope to achieve?
What do you hope to ignite?

Your intention should be roughly a sentence long and it signifies what you are doing and why. Suggestions to help create your intention might be:

What do I want/ need right now?
What do I hope to feel/ receive from this ritual?

Once you have answered the above, create an intention with one sentence. For example:

"Today I ask for peace/ I call in peace."
"I am asking for help to change . . ."
"This ritual is to learn how to move forward in my life."

Sacred Space:
Your sacred space is an area you define to be spiritual where you can call upon the Universal Energies to harness. We explored how to set up your sacred altar in the previous section on page 109.

To commence your ritual, open your sacred space by taking a few deep breaths and finding a way that resonates with you to signify the beginning of it. I suggested earlier about lighting a candle; I also like to ring a bell. Some people place their hands in prayer as they breathe, some say "aum," others burn incense or sage. Do whatever resonates with you and try to get into the habit of doing it to signal that the ritual has commenced. The reason I say get into a habit of it is because this "beginning" creates a specific vibration within you, which when recreated repetitively reminds you of what is to come. Your memory remembers this vibration with a certain level of awareness, and with time it grows deeper and stronger. When igniting rituals and calling upon the energies of the unconscious world we need to be in a deep state of presence, non-attachment and awareness, so the more we signal the beginning, the easier it will be to get into this mind frame.

Look to your symbolic items for the Universal Energy and allow yourself to be drawn around your sacred space as you wish. In Shamanism many set up their sacred altar in a formation like a cross, which they call the four directions or a medicine wheel. In Witchcraft, the elements are usually arranged in the tip points of the pentagon star. This ritual is your own creation, so create it as you wish. There is no wrong or right way to do it.

As you move through the elements, remind yourself what they represent and call upon their energy to be present. I like to say variations of the below:

I call upon the spirits of the east, Fire Energy. Bring forth your blessings to open this sacred space. May the warmth of your flames illuminate our hearts and protect us in this sacred space as we journey to the unseen realms to ignite this ritual.

I call upon the spirits of the south, Water Energy. Come forth with your guidance to allow life to flow in harmony with the cosmic tides of the Universe. May we feel your beautiful currents soothe our emotions as we embark upon this ritual.

I call upon the spirits of the west, Great Mother Earth Energy. May we feel the nurturing love of our ancestors and the divine creation of life. Keep us grounded as we navigate this space, and open our hearts to your unconditional love.

I call upon the spirits of the north, Air Energy. May you come forth and bring peace to our minds as you guide us gently through these vibrations into a place of love and safety. I open myself to receiving your blessings as you bring clarity over this ritual space.

And I call upon the spirits of our ancestors, Grandfather Sun, Grandmother Moon, the spirits of the Great Divine, our Spirit Guides, and Spirit Animals. Please come forth and bless this space as we release and surrender anything that is holding us back from believing our truth. Thank you for walking alongside me as I invite in only positive vibrations; thank you for your protection and for your loving light energy.

Now that we have set up our sacred space and called upon the energies, it is time for us to speak our intention loudly. We then reiterate our intention by formulating an action to support it.

Action:
A physical motion of doing something to implement the intention, for example, meditating, journaling, creating, or singing.

You can integrate any form of meditation into your ritual. My favorite meditation to add during a ritual is creative visualization. To do this, whilst in a meditative state, envision yourself journeying to the unseen realms and harness the desired goal or energy that relates to your intention. You could achieve this by reciting your intention and seeing it as a manifested consciousness, either through an image, or a feeling of what it would be to live it out in your reality. If your intention was an action, imagine yourself playing it out. Allow the energy of what it is to completely consume you so that you are influencing your body to experience this vibration, thus bringing it closer into your reality.

Other ideas to ignite a strong ritual action include:

Getting creative. Use art and craft to create and embody the energy of your intention. Allow a vision to come through to you and hold no boundaries, no limits on what you can create.

Create a potion. Gather your favorite leaves, twigs, flowers from the garden and create something with it. With each item you place into your bowl or sacred space call in its energy, ask for its blessing, give thanks to its presence.

Try to implement a ritual into your life daily. Find something that you enjoy that brings you peace, that connects your attention to the present moment, and allows you to journey to the unseen realms without interruption.

Once you have completed your ritual, spend some time journaling to reflect on how you currently feel and how your life is flowing for you right now. Try to pinpoint where you can create change for yourself and support your intention to come into your reality.

What am I already doing that brings this intention into my life?
What can I do more of?
What can I do less of?

An example of this could be that you want more peace and happiness in your life. But what are you doing to provide yourself with peace and happiness? How often do you spend time doing the things that bring you those feelings? What are you doing that doesn't bring you peace and happiness? It all stems back to the "who am I?" questions of what it is that brings joy to my soul. And if you have clarity over this, what about getting to the core of who you are as a person. Do you know who you are, and are you showing this version of yourself to the world?

Journaling, self-reflection, and meditation are a crucial part of your ritual process for this is how you connect with your intuition and learn the wisdom of how to bring forth the vibrations that you seek.

Closure:

To close your ritual follow through with a similar process to how you opened it. As you honor each of the Universal Energies, give gratitude for their presence and wisdom. Recite your intention again but this time say it as though it is done, or in an affirmation format. Perhaps you asked for guidance at the beginning of the ritual, so now to close your circle you would say, "I now hold the wisdom of how to move forward, and that is through ..." Reiterate the knowledge learned so that you have pulled the energy of the unconscious into your conscious realm.

Choose an action to symbolize the end of your ritual, such as if you lit a candle, blow it out, or ring a bell or chimes, or take a deep breath in and out. Simply the words, "this ritual is now closed" suffices too.

We will explore many rituals throughout this book, with a specific focus on healing. Many of the other subjects that we explore which hold journaling questions also allow for a ritual to be created beforehand, so have fun experimenting and exploring how to do this yourself based off the suggestions in the previous passages.

Self-Love

Self-love is the pathway to our greatest success. We cannot achieve anything in this life until we master the act of self-love unto ourselves. Yet, this idea of self-love is never spoken about in school, nor the importance of it communicated to us at a young age. If self-love was openly conversed imagine all the problems in the world that could disappear? Mental health, body image issues, low-self-esteem, feeling unloved from parents or family. So many issues could be healed if we just learned how to bring love to ourselves first.

To help understand the importance of self-love, let's look at the following example:

Imagine that you are holding a basket full of flowers. If you learn how to go out into the field and pick your own flowers to fill your basket up, you will always have plenty of flowers for yourself and extra flowers to share generously with others. If you learn how to fill your own basket up you will be able to choose whatever color, texture, and type of flower you want to carry, encouraging feelings of empowerment and confidence for you can control what kind and how many flowers you choose to collect. But if you don't take the time to learn how to fill your own basket up, you will be forced to latch onto other people, asking for their flowers, trying to fulfill something that can never be fulfilled from another. Because your basket isn't full you will be desperate in your choices and you won't be able to pick and choose which flowers you want to gather. The energy you emit will be that of scarcity and you will attract other low vibrational people into your life. Some people will only give you flowers with conditions attached and others may give flowers that don't smell, or look pretty or do anything at all. And deep inside you will feel hollow and empty.

The basket represents your heart, and the flowers are the loving and happy vibrations. If you focus on creating your own love and happiness, you will be overflowing with this beautiful energy and can attract other like-minded individuals, whilst giving lavishly without depleting your energy. But if you don't take the time to look after yourself you will try to harness any vibration possible, thus attracting all sorts of energy. When we fill ourselves up with self-love, we have more love to others give in return.

Through self-love we create peace in our lives and harmony in the world. The spiritual path isn't just about "finding the positive," it's about being truthful, raw, and honest with ourselves, revealing the darkness and honoring it in the same depth that we do the light.

Asking questions such as:
What's going on in me right now?
How does this make me feel?
How can I improve myself and my life?

So what exactly is self-love, and why is it so important?
To love yourself completely is to accept yourself exactly as you are right in this very moment. Understand that you have been gifted all the tools you need for this life and that your soul chose this body, this mind, and this journey. Self-love is learning to respect your time, your space, your abilities, and your limits. It's to acknowledge what you are good at, what you aren't so good at, and encouraging yourself to be better.

What does it feel like to love yourself?
When you love yourself, you are mindful in all that you do. Your health is at its optimum best because you care about everything that you put into your body. You eat nutritious food that is beneficial to

the support of your health. You exercise regularly, not necessarily vigorously, but enough to help the functionality of your body, and get your heart rate moving. You enjoy spending time alone, doing the things that you love to honor your soul as you allow your creativity to dance freely in your reality. You fill your days with purpose, listening to the voice of your intuition speak loudly as you do all the things that your soul craves. You adhere to your boundaries and know yourself exceptionally well. You do all of these things because you know that when you serve love to yourself first, you are able to give more love to others in return. When you love yourself you set the standard of love and respect that you deserve.

When we love ourselves we have patience with our time and we have faith that everything in our life is aligned as it should be. When we love ourselves we never act or do anything that harm our self-love. We don't self-sabotage, for we know our self-worth and we have high self-esteem. We don't succumb to addictions, or abuse our body in any way. Because we love ourselves, we respect ourselves, we are kind to ourselves, we only want the best for ourselves and from this space we lead the way to educate others on how they should treat us too. The more love we give to ourselves, the more love we generate in return. When we give love to ourselves we vibrate a higher frequency and this vibration is a magnet to invite in beautiful experiences and attract like-minded people.

Self-Love Mirror Exercise

Mirror reflections are a great introduction to understand the way you feel about yourself. The purpose of this exercise is to become comfortable with your body and face to open up the doorway into practice loving yourself. You need to see how incredibly beautiful you are, and what better way to do this than by looking in the mirror! These mirror exercises are also a form of positive self-talk. You need to be comfortable giving your own advice and listening to yourself because you hold the answer to every question you could ever ask.

1. Find a mirror where you can be alone and look at yourself directly in the eyes.

2. Recite whichever affirmation feels right to you (or both).
   "I love you" or "I love myself."

3. Repeat this self-love affirmation at least three times with a deep breath in between. Be sincere.

4. Allow any thoughts to arise from this experience, whether negative or positive.

5. Get a journal and answer the following questions:

How do I feel when I say these words?
Did I believe that what I was saying was true?
If not, what's holding me back from not believing it?
What can I do to help myself overcome this?

Take a moment to write down your feelings and thoughts. Do this exercise often, starting with your eyes and face, and then moving to other areas of your body where you want to love and accept yourself. Notice any changes in your life from doing this exercise (write them down). Remind yourself that you deserve to give love to yourself and that you are worthy of receiving this love.

Self-Love Journal Exercise

Open your journal to a fresh page and write today's date at the top. Write down the following sentence and take note of how you feel as you do so.

I love myself.

Write down how you felt when you wrote it.
Did any sensations arrive in your body as you wrote it down?
Do you agree, or disagree with the statement?

If you agree, write down five things that you love about yourself.
I love myself because . . .

If you disagree, write down why you disagree with this statement.
I don't love myself because . . .

As you look at the list above, imagine it were a friend saying this to you. What would you say in reply?
Why are the above statements not true?
How can you turn those negatives thoughts into positive statements so that you can move to a place of acceptance?

What is my relationship with myself like?
Do I look after myself?
Do I listen to myself?
Am I kind to myself?
How can I work on myself more?
How do I love myself?
What things do I do that prove that I love myself?

Maybe you love your skin and so having a long bath and putting lotion on your body makes you happy. Or you like nature, so you have a plant at home that you look after, or perhaps you go for walks in nature. But how often are you doing these things? Do you do them every day, or once a week?

Where do I feel I am lacking love for myself?
How can I improve on this?

An example of this might be that you are not gifting yourself enough time to be alone and enjoy your own company. If you don't like being on your own, that's a drastic calling for self-love. Alone time is your time of sanctuary, your place of happiness, of peace and tranquil. This is where you gather your energy from and honor yourself.

Write down what activities make you happy:
Choose two or more activities you enjoy doing at home.
Choose two or more activities you enjoy doing outside.
Choose two or more activities you enjoy doing with other people.
And from this list, make an effort to incorporate one of these activities each day.

Examples can be something like: having a bath, going for a walk, cooking, even playing dress-ups with yourself is a form of positive time alone for you are getting comfortable with your presence. Anything that encourages a positive self-image is an act of self-love.

What makes you feel good about yourself? Maybe you like listening to music, singing, dancing, or painting. Set time aside this week, put it in the calendar—"make time for play"—and make some suggestions on how to support this.

Playtime is important to partake in regularly as it reduces stress, allows energy to be released, encourages positive connections with others, and inspires your creativity to flow freely. Play enables us to focus our awareness onto the experience of life, the positive emotions we are able to derive and express from our own doing which is empowering! It also encourages a light-hearted outlook on life and not to take ourselves or life too seriously. Our goal is to enjoy and experience! Playtime can be socializing with friends, playing with animals, or creative expressions of drawing and painting. Anything that allows yourself to be living in the present moment and enjoying that moment!

But playtime doesn't just have to be exclusive to actions with others; it's important to learn how to love being on our own too, and finding what it is that we are good at, to reinforce the positive areas of our life.

Write down five things you are good at doing.
These can be as little or as big as you like. They can be an action, or a feeling of appreciation. They must be something positive.
Examples:
I am wonderful at cooking.
I excel at finding the best restaurants to eat at.
I have a talent at making people feel good about themselves.
I have a beautiful smile.

Understanding and accepting ourselves is crucial to self-love. If you don't like yourself, how do you expect other people to like you?

By understanding your strengths and weaknesses, you open the doors to self-improvement and manage your own expectations. Through understanding yourself, you will be prepared for the world's challenges. For you will be able to identify your strongest coping mechanism, your way of seeking peace, and learn how to handle situations the right way. Through loving yourself, you can calm your mind and learn how to perceive situations from a different perspective to create the peace around you that you seek.

In the same respect that we acknowledge our positive attributes, we need to do the same with our weaknesses. Weaknesses are not always a negative trait. It's good to know your own limitations and to not be pessimistic about them because everyone has them! Self-love is accepting ourselves exactly as we are. When we are aware of our weaknesses we can make better decisions that support our needs. We can predetermine how best to support ourselves to achieve our goals by knowing our strengths and weaknesses. We know that if we have difficulty with something we can ask someone for help or educate ourselves to try and be better.

With each weakness write down something positive after it, i.e.
I'm not a great swimmer, but I'm trying and I might be one day.
I'm not great at climbing but I prefer hiking and I'm good at it.
I'm quite introvert so being in social gatherings makes me feel uncomfortable, but when people talk to me, I'm a great listener.

By knowing our strengths and weaknesses we are able to create a life that we feel comfortable with that provides us with an opportunity to excel in. Our strengths and weaknesses are what makes us unique and different. So today, work through your strengths and weaknesses and accept yourself exactly as you are, because right now, you are perfect.

It's important to self-reflect over every area of your life, so that you have a clear vision of the kind of person you are and the kind of love that you are giving and receiving. Let's examine the people you surround yourself with.

Who are the people in your life who accept you for you, and inspire you to be the greatest version of yourself?
How often do you speak to these people?
How often do you spend time with these people?
What is it that you like about them?
Why are they an important part of your life?
Do you reciprocate the same level of energy to them?
The qualities that you see in them, do they see them in you?

The qualities that you find in the people who you choose to surround yourself with will be the qualities that you will automatically attract and adapt into your own character, so it's important that these people are good people.

Choose one person in your list and make an effort to connect with this person. Contact them in person, or via phone or email.

If you found it difficult to answer this question of having a person in your life as a role model, that's okay. You are not alone. We are building the tools to help you attract the right people into your life. It's only a matter of time before your group of positive lightworkers will arrive.

Acceptance of Self-Affirmation:
I accept where I am in my life right now.
Everything is perfectly on time and aligned.
I am right where I need to be.
I am doing the best I know how to.
I accept myself in this moment right now.

Self-love and self-acceptance is a feeling, not a logical concept to understand. It comes from the accumulation of the little things— knowing when to say no, giving yourself "me" time and not feeling guilty about it. Self-love supports feeding yourself with nourishing food and exercising regularly. Self-love is leaving bad relationships, defining strong boundaries, and rewarding yourself for your accomplishments.

Aim to journal every day and self-reflect over your life. Asking questions such as:

Am I acting in alignment with my beliefs?

Have I removed bad relationships from my life?

Am I communicating my boundaries and saying no as needed?

Am I listening to what my heart truly wants?

Am I allowing my soul to dance through my creativity?

When you love yourself it becomes an organic process to continue feeding yourself that love. For you will become more confident and walk with high respect for yourself and everyone who surrounds you. From this space, there's no other option than for life to flow harmoniously in peace. And when our life is flowing we can co-create our destiny with the power of the Universe.

The more love we give ourselves the more pleasurable our life becomes. This is the secret to living a happy and successful life, by learning how to live authentically and sharing that authenticity with the world. You have a unique gift to share and the only way to share this is by doing the work to learn how to love, honor and praise your soul. Self love is the first step toward this journey.

Boundaries

Setting boundaries is an important act of self-love.

If we do not establish and communicate our boundaries it emits the impression that we don't respect ourselves and in turn, gives people permission to take advantage of us. By creating boundaries we are honoring ourselves. When you communicate your boundaries you are showing people how to love you, because you are setting the example through loving yourself first.

But what exactly are boundaries? Boundaries can be defined as a series of beliefs that adhere to what you deem to be acceptable behavior and a code of ethics from other people and your relationships with them.

For example, in a romantic relationship, perhaps you consider emotional cheating and physical cheating as the same thing. Both are forms of being unfaithful, and you do not accept this in your relationship. A boundary could be:
"I don't wish to participate in an open relationship, and any kind of cheating is unacceptable."

In a friendship, perhaps you feel as though you are giving and never receiving in return. You need to be vocal in explaining that this is not acceptable behavior to you. Therefore, a boundary could be:
"I expect equal time and effort to be shared in a friendship; it should be a fair exchange of energy."

Boundaries are important to protect your energy. When a situation arises or a person acts in a way that makes you feel uncomfortable and doesn't align with your values, your beliefs and/or insults your self-love or self-respect, this is when it is time to set a boundary to stop that behavior. It's important to stand strong by your boundary, despite another person's opinion. You must also agree that everyone deserves the same respect and equal right to their own boundaries. We are all different and just because we think differently doesn't mean that one person is superior to another. But the more we voice our needs and wants the more we will find the right people who agree and support our ideas and boundaries; this is how we find our loyal circle of friends and encourage happiness into our lives.

Creating Your Own Boundaries

To create your own list of boundaries get your journal and let's explore what you determine ethical behavior is.

What kind of behavior do I believe is acceptable?

What kind of behavior do I believe is unacceptable?

Examples of unacceptable behavior could be gossiping, putting others down, dishonesty, selfish/ hurtful behavior.

Are there any people or situations in my life whose behavior is unacceptable or unethical?

What type of people do I hope to surround myself with?

Do any of my friends have these qualities?

What kind of friendships do I want to have together?

Envision the kind of relationship you want to have with someone in particular. It could be a friend, partner, family, or work relationship, or repeat this exercise for all four.

Imagine the kind of feeling you would love to share when you spend time with this person and write it down.

Imagine the kind of conversation you would like to have with this person and write it down.

From this exercise you're envisioning your ideal life with the kind of people you wish to surround yourself with who will complement your own happiness and peace.

According to the above, write down a few (or many) boundaries that you choose to live by. Are there any situations that do not align with these values? Are there any people in your life who don't adhere to these boundaries? If yes, make a conscious effort to remove these people from your life. You can be vocal in your decision if you feel comfortable communicating it, or instead energetically remove yourself and stop sharing a lot of time with them.

Suggested List of Boundaries

- It's okay to say no and not feel guilty
- It's okay for others to disagree with me
- I have a right to feel safe and respected
- I am responsible for my own happiness
- It's not my responsibility to make others happy
- I have the freedom to choose my lifestyle choices
- I'm allowed to express my opinions, needs, and feelings
- I give myself permission to be unapologetically me
- I am enough exactly as I am, right in this moment

It's okay to say no and not feel guilty

Have you ever felt like you're living someone else's life? That you keep agreeing to seeing people or to do things that don't feel right for you but you do it because you feel guilty, or bored, or you don't want to hurt someone else's feelings? Those are the things you need to say no to and not feel guilty about. When we know ourselves we can prioritize our own needs first. Because when we come from this place of internal contentment and fulfillment, we are in a much stronger position to give more in return. Otherwise you will exhaust yourself trying to please everyone else. Learning to say no without guilt, shame, or fear is very empowering. Your soul will thank you for it. Saying yes to the things you don't want to do is only hurting yourself.

It's okay for others to disagree with me

You have a right to express your opinions and decisions. You do not have to ask permission for anything (granted that you are not hurting someone or doing something illegal). When you make decisions from a place of love, and in alignment with who you are, you cannot be upset if someone doesn't agree with you. And it's not up to anyone else but you. Own your opinions and your choices because denying them will only deny the voice of your soul. We are all uniquely different and this is what encourages change in the world. As long as you are not hurting anyone, be proud of your difference of opinion.

I have a right to feel safe and respected

Everyone is entitled to safety and respect. It's up to you to make sure you give and receive this basic human right. Resorting to victimizing cries and assuming that it's someone else's job to do this for you will not solve anything. This kind of attitude is giving your power away and it is the quickest pathway to unhappiness. Safety and respect is a right that every living creature on the planet deserves and if you do not have this from your closest friends and family, make a choice to look elsewhere and give this safety and respect to yourself.

I am responsible for my own happiness
You deserve happiness. You are worthy of love. Everything that makes you happy is attainable to you, but it's up to you to make it happen. It's your responsibility to go after what you want and to get what you want. Once you figure out what it is that makes you happy, it's your responsibility and yours alone to ensure that this happiness is created. Never blame someone else for whatever is happening in your world, because you own your reactions and actions and from these two places you can create the happiness and peace that you seek; you just need to open your mind and change your perspective.

It's not my responsibility to make others happy
I know it's frustrating when you see how much they are hurting themselves. But you have to just keep going and be the best version of yourself, hope that they come around, but know that if they don't that it's their path, not yours. All we can do is lead by example, and encourage others to do the same. It's not your role to tell them how to live their life (unless they are causing harm to you or themselves). We must respect everyone's journey. We must be open to understanding that everyone is learning their own way. Everyone is acting according to their level of understanding and awareness. It is not your job to direct or give advice unless asked for. And if you are asked, place no expectations for others to listen or act as you request. It can be frustrating when you see others in pain when the solution is so clear but they won't do it, because they are acting according to their level of awareness and they will change their ways in their own time. We cannot rush another nor criticize them for taking longer. We are all on our own life path and life journey.

I have the freedom to choose my lifestyle choices

Just as we allow everyone around us to choose their lifestyle choices, you deserve the same respect. Give yourself permission to love who you want, to do what you want, to be who you want. You can live however you desire in a way that makes you happy. Of course, this is assuming that you are not hurting others at your own expense of happiness. Perhaps there is some confusion with hurting others - so I would like to be specific. By hurting others with your lifestyle decisions, I mean physically or emotionally harming them, or, if you are harming yourself. Choices such as a drug lifestyle, a lifestyle where you don't respect another person. These negative behavior patterns are not acceptable and professional help is recommended.

I'm allowed to express my opinions, needs, and feelings

Your unique voice is crucial to the world. Your ideas and beliefs are important. The more we share our thoughts and feelings the more connected we become thus creating a brighter future for all, ensuring that everyone is included and looked after. Your opinions, needs, and feelings are validated. If something isn't right in your life, use everything that you can to make it known and to change it. You don't need to wait for someone to tell you it's okay for you to ask for something, because this is your life and if you want something, you go and get it. You deserve everything that you want and more!

I give myself permission to be unapologetically me

You are worthy of living the life that you want. In order to create this life, you need to be yourself. You need to speak your truth and share your unique point of view. If you hold yourself back from being true to yourself your soul will suffer, and you will be disappointed in yourself and look at your life with great sadness. Be unapologetically you without needing another's permission or approval. When we are true to ourselves, we step closer into alignment with our Higher Self.

I am enough exactly as I am, right in this moment

You are and have always been enough. You are always growing, changing and adapting and that's what makes you beautiful. Who you are today is not who you were yesterday, and it's not who you are going to be tomorrow. And each of those versions of yourself is enough. Because you are you. And just simply being you is enough. You don't have to try and be more than what you already are because you already are perfect. You are living the life you are meant to; everything in your life is right on time. You don't need to do a thing because you are and have always been enough.

The love and respect that you give yourself and the boundaries you choose also need to be reciprocated. You also need to give others the same respect for their boundaries. Everything is an equal exchange of energy and no person is more superior than another.

A Personal Story on Boundaries:
Learning how to say no was my strongest boundary lesson I needed to master. I had a deep-rooted insecurity for the need to people please. I had issues when people didn't like me, I didn't understand. Shouldn't everyone like me? *was my belief. That was the first mistake I should have tackled! No, not everyone is going to like you, because not everyone likes themselves. Once I learned that people not liking or accepting me had more to do with their own problems and insecurities, as opposed to mine, I was able to let go of constantly striving to people please. I was able to say no and not feel guilty, realizing that saying no was actually a strength for it showed that I valued my own time and it proved that I knew myself. I was saying no because it wasn't right for me, not to be difficult, not because I was scared, but because I simply didn't want to. What a powerful word to use when known how! I also want to add that it's important to know how to say no graciously. It doesn't hurt to be kind when saying no, as long as you aren't sacrificing yourself at the same time.*

Body + Spirituality

We explored self-love in relation to our personality, actions, decisions, beliefs, but what about love for our body and face? In order to completely harmonize the flow of energy between our mind, body, and soul we need to love and accept ourselves exactly as we are right in this moment.

You are given one body to use, and not just any body, your soul chose this body for a reason. And if in this moment of time you find yourself struggling to accept your body, or perhaps it is working against you, remind yourself that you can overcome anything! You have the ability to love and heal your body. You just need to be patient to learn how your body works at its optimum prime and to do this you need to examine every area of your life. You have control over what you feed your body and how to nurture your body, but you first need to become friends with your body to learn what it is that your body needs.

What food makes your body thrive?
What exercise complements your physique?
Are you feeding your body with loving thoughts as well as nutritious food?
Do you engage in light exercise to ensure your organs and muscles are able to work at their ultimate level?

The answer of what to feed your body differs for everyone, but at the core basis of everything, it is scientifically proven that a well-balanced plant-based diet will always overrule. And the term "well-balanced" is the key here. You need to eat a variety of nuts, seeds, legumes, vegetables, and fruit. The moment that meat is eliminated from our diet our body has the ability and liberty to work to its optimum level. Our human bodies are not designed to eat meat. We aren't born with sharp teeth or claw-like nails that enables us to kill. Our digestive system is more complex than other carnivore animals; our intestines are longer and we do not hold the same acidity which means that meat takes an unhealthy length of time to pass through our digestive system causing it to rot and for harmful bacteria to breed. Eating meat and dairy not only attributes to digestive issues but also to long-term illnesses and disease. When we remove meat and dairy from our body we are able to create a pure temple to host our soul. The cleaner our internal organs become, the more efficient our body will be, and from here we will be able to understand how to care and learn for ourselves. When we have a clean body we are able to hear the voice of our body and listen to what it needs. Just like our intuition tells us what our soul needs, our body has the ability to do so also.

Eating a well-balanced plant-based diet also encourages us to actually learn about the food we eat and what it is that we are fueling our bodies with. The first reason we eat is for survival and the second is for our own pleasure. However, many people have these two purposes mixed around the opposite way. Once we learn about the food we eat and how it benefits us we are able to combine both objectives effortlessly, providing more joy and meaning to our every mouthful.

Eating a plant-based diet benefits not only your body and your mind, but also the environment around you. The reason our planet is in such turmoil today is largely due to the overpopulation of animals that we unnecessarily breed for consumption. We are brainwashed from large corporations to believe that eating meat and dairy is a necessity to provide nutrients to our body, yet this is scientifically incorrect. When you eat a well-balanced plant-based diet you receive an abundance of nutrients and vitamins, in the most healthiest way possible. But when you consume meat and dairy, you receive less powerful nutrients, covered in fat and disease.

Not only is a plant-based diet better for our bodies to work at their best self, but the consumption of meat and dairy directly relates to disease in the body. Every disease that we create is the result of a poor diet, or stress (mind), and usually it's a combination of both. We cannot eliminate diseases in our life without addressing these two factors: what we eat and what we think. By focusing on purifying our thoughts with meditation and eating plant-based foods we harmonize the flow of energy between our mind and body, thus enabling ourselves to live a long and healthy life.

Eating a plant-based diet is also linked with living a spiritual life and to explain this we need to examine the energy that is held in a slaughtered animal. We know that at the core of every living thing are atoms that vibrate and radiate energy. This energy radiates at different frequencies and depending on what emotions are derived from our being will determine the frequency range we emit. A happy and peaceful living organism will vibrate at a much higher frequency than those who are sad or sick. Not only are animals kept against their will in confined spaces whilst living in inhumane conditions in order to breed for mass production, but they are slaughtered and disregarded brutally. In the last moments of their life the animals feel terror, fear, and anger. That specific energy frequency is trapped inside the animal upon death and when you eat it, you too are consuming this depleted and negative energy into your own body.

When you eat plant-based foods you are eating food that is still alive, and you are consuming nutrients in a way that cannot be achieved from dead animals. Furthermore, fruit and vegetables are filled with seeds which are the source of life itself. Not only are you eating many layers of beneficial nutrients, you are eating the creator of life!

The lack of veganism in the world comes down to a lack of education. We are rarely given the tools needed to educate ourselves properly because why would we when there's so much money being made by keeping us ignorant? While we are so busy focusing on surviving, we place our trust in others, and rightly so, for we are weaving the web of our future together. But unfortunately, not everyone has the population's best interest at heart and we can see this by the lethal chain in place to encourage money and mass production in the meat and dairy industry.

The meat and dairy industry pay for marketing and advertising that falsely claim health benefits, whilst ignoring the toxicity of the actual product. The advertising companies are happy to receive a large sum of money so they say yes to running the ads, even though these very ads are a key part of the problem for they are the reason for the miseducation. The meat and dairy eaters then find themselves very sick and turn to Western doctors who usually prescribe pills for the new diseases that their body has created in response from eating other animal diseases. Some of the doctors receive money from the pharmaceutical companies depending on what products they prescribe, regardless of the evidence of that product working and so we are receiving miseducation from both sides. We then turn to the charities for guidance only to research deeply and learn that many of them are also funded by the meat and dairy industry and pharmaceutical companies. The data is fabricated to reflect a bias opinion to encourage sales and growth of individual companies, leaving the consumer behind to suffer the consequences. And it continues in a vicious cycle.

The meat and dairy industry is making us sick, but when we ask our doctors not enough of them will tell us to change our diet; instead, they prescribe pills to mask the problem because they get more money from the pharmaceutical companies this way. The research centers who find the cause and reasons why the disease has arrived in our body is also funded by the meat and dairy industry so they can't tell you the truth about your diet either. The news and media platforms who we turn to for education are also paid by these large corporations to advertise their products and so they will never say anything bad about their highest-paying clients! It becomes very difficult to find out the truth because there will never be a bad word published about them in the news or media, or if there are any opposing voices (from independent sources who do not gain money by lying), the articles will be squashed and combated so that the truth stays hidden. This isn't the first time we have seen large companies pay out doctors, media and research centers to support their own benefit to advertise false information legally, just research about the tobacco and sugar industry to find out more.

The reason why a lot of this turmoil exists is due to lack of education. Many Western doctors are rarely taught how to treat patients with food and natural medicine because they don't learn enough of this at university. For this reason we are seeing a tremendous growth of naturopaths, and nutritionists to help others heal through food. Our bodies were designed to heal themselves. We need to get out of the way, stop feeding ourselves unnatural food that holds no nutrients and start feeding ourselves soul-nurturing food gifted from Mother Earth. Start listening to your body, and make a choice to take back your power, heal yourself. Stop giving your power away!

When you begin to incorporate plant-based meals into your life you will notice immediate changes in your mood and energy. As you continue eating a well-balanced plan-based diet you will be able to understand your body in a way like never before. You will be able to tell if a food is beneficial or detrimental to your health because through your own observation your body will be signaling what it needs and wants and you will be able to hear it speak loudly. The more consistent you are with listening to your body, the better you will feel and the more productive you will be. After many months of a plant-based lifestyle you will start to see things differently. Your perception of the world will be changed as you will now appreciate and praise all the living creatures around you which is beneficial to your mind, body, and soul, as it promotes the feeling of connectedness that we aspire to as explored in spiritual philosophy #2 (page 142). Examining our relationship with food will provide a deeper level of fulfillment. We have normalized the killing of animals so much in this world that we have become numb to what is really happening before us. If everyone in the world saw the horrific environments that animals were forced to live in there would be a great deal more vegan eaters on the planet.

My Personal Story of Switching to a Plant-Based Diet

My relationship with food was traumatic in my late adolescence. From the ages of 17 - 21, no matter what I fed my body, it rejected it. After every single meal I would be in agony. My stomach would erupt with excruciating cramps for at least an hour until the food passed through my body. Over the period of five years I saw every doctor possible in the hope to reveal the reason as to why I was unable to digest food. Conventional doctors, naturopaths, nutritionists, allergy specialists, and the list goes on. But no one could figure it out. One naturopath suggested a gluten intolerance. To which I promptly followed a gluten-free diet—however, at this time, gluten-free products didn't exist and to try and create a diet that supported this meal plan was difficult for a young girl. Things began to improve for a few months (as they did with each diet I tried), but then either a new symptom would develop or my stomach would reject the food in the same agonizing way as before. Except now I would have even more confusion and anger toward my body. I was scared of being social and sharing meals with friends, unsure of how my body would react. And my own eating became a boring ordeal of trying to find something that my stomach actually liked. My skin was irritated, I felt bloated all the time. I felt like I was allergic to everything! But when I had my allergies tested everything came back normal! The only thing that the Western doctor could determine was that I was anemic. But taking iron supplements created huge stomach congestion, and I couldn't take them. So by this stage I had been suffering with difficulty digesting food (also absorbing nutrients), I had an iron deficiency, and felt tired all the time. And no one could help figure out what was wrong or how to heal.

It wasn't until I learned about a vegan diet that my life changed forever. I had tried every diet suggested by these doctors, but not one had ever suggested a vegan diet! I had reached a point of having nothing to lose and so I thought let's give it a go. I knew it would be challenging, but I was hopeful, and so I decided to test out a plant-based diet for three months to see how I felt. The first week was the hardest. I had been so conditioned to think that a meal revolved around meat, I had no idea how to prepare my meal. And so, the beginning of unlearning what I thought I knew began. I educated myself about the food that I was feeding into my body, making sure I was nurturing and filling my body with what it needed. Eating out was harder than being gluten free! The servers looked at me weirdly when asking for a vegan option, and when I did receive a meal it was basically just a plate minus the meat; no one really knew how to facilitate for a vegan diet. Luckily, this is beginning to change in many cities around the world, but I still find it difficult to eat at restaurants, there is still so much more that needs to be learned! The second week was a true test of discipline. It's not that I craved meat at all, but I craved food, and the extra time spent researching about the food I was eating, learning how to make interesting recipes, all took time and dedication, but still, I was committed. It wasn't until the fourth week that my whole life changed. My energy levels had increased completely, my iron deficiency had vanished (blood tests proved this), even the white of my eyes were bright again. I realized that not once since I changed to a plant-based diet was my stomach upset. Not once was I in agony! That was a huge revelation! I had been almost scared of food for five years. And finally, finally, finally - I learned what it was that my body needed within four weeks! I finally understood my body; I worked with my body, not against it. I was listening to my body. And my body wanted vegan!

At the time of writing this book I've been plant-based for 15 years and I have never eaten meat or seafood since. Not once! I've never craved it, never missed it. Each step along the way has helped to evolve my own understanding of the food I am eating and how I am nurturing and nourishing my body. My body is so clean that the moment I eat something that it doesn't like (usually something processed), my body will let me know immediately. I am still gluten free (vegan and gluten free is a difficult combination, but it is getting better). My understanding of gluten free is dependent on what country I go to, for it's the way that food is processed differently and the preservatives that are included in it. Although my vegan journey began with diet and nutrition, it has evolved dramatically to reflect other areas of my life. I am now cautious in making a conscious effort to buy vegan and sustainable clothes, shoes, bags, and skincare. My connection with animals has grown deeper than ever before. I don't see a piece of meat on a plate like a meat-eater does, I see the animal, I see the heart that was once beating. I feel more aligned with the natural flow of life. And most importantly, my mind, body, and soul feel in harmony. Food doesn't become a problem, it's simplified. I feel empowered because I know what I'm eating and the gift that food is giving me. When changing to a plant-based diet it's important to understand what you're eating and how it nurtures your body. You must spend time educating yourself and learning how to feed yourself. Speak to a health expert and learn how to incorporate a well-balanced diet into your life.

How to Eat Mindfully

1. Remove any electronics from your awareness as you eat. These purposely distract you, changing your mood and emotions.

2. Take five long, deep breaths in and out before you eat.

3. Look at the food you are about to eat and make sure that you understand what it is that you are eating. If it is baked or processed, how was it created? What are the nutrients you are receiving and where does that food come from? It's important to educate yourself about the benefits that you are feeding your body and internal system so that you can make smarter and healthier eating choices. It takes time to learn this, but like anything, it is knowledge that you will carry with you always.

4. After you eat, take note of how you feel. Do you feel too full? Did you eat something your body didn't like? Keep a journal of certain foods you enjoy and their benefits to ensure that you are providing yourself with the best nutrients possible.

You want to fill your plate with "alive" foods (which are foods that are close to their natural organic form), because these are the foods that provide the most benefits. Avoid "dead food" such as man made products, and animal products. As you become more connected with the food you consume, the link between yourself and your body will deepen, encouraging an awareness as to what your body needs and doesn't like. You will finally learn the language of your body and how to support it to be the greatest version of yourself.

When learning about specific foods and what they provide to you, some studies have shown that foods that look like body parts ironically provide the most benefit to that specific body part. Examples of this are: Walnuts are good for brain. Carrots are good for eyes. Celery is good for our bone development. Avocados are good for the uterus. Kidney beans are good for the kidneys. Grapefruit benefits our breasts. If you have an area of your body that you know is weak, ensure to learn the best plant-based product that supports that organ or muscle and incorporate it into your diet. Keep a journal to document your own progression.

Emotional eating is a common problem linked to over and/or under eating. This is why it's important to eat mindfully every time, and make sure that we keep our mental health nurtured and nourished. Food and diet plays a vital role in our mental health, and deficiencies in vitamins and nutrients can lead to depression or anxiety so it's important to eat a well-balanced diet at all times. When you are eating you are fueling your body. This time is sacred. You are feeding energy to your body and helping it thrive. Make your meals delicious every time that you eat and allow your emotions to be pleasured. Taking your time to chew your food properly is also important for this is where your food is best digested.

As you incorporate a vegan diet into your lifestyle, you will feel more connected and confident with your body and in turn be able to understand and listen to it more. Which will bring forth a deeper connection to self-acceptance and self-love. We are here to work with our body, not against it. A plant-based lifestyle is the only diet that has proven to be the most beneficial form of nutrition whilst maintaining a healthy weight when consumed correctly. A plant-based diet is scientifically proven to prevent and heal disease, and it is the secret to a long and vibrant life.

Just because someone is vegan it doesn't mean they are healthy. Cutting out meat is just the beginning; you need to understand what exactly it is that you are putting into your body, and educate yourself about the food that you are eating. It's not just about the big corporations that are winning as a result of you consuming their products and getting sick. It's about you learning to fuel your body with the most efficient nutrients so that you may perform at an optimum level.

Eating a healthy diet is just the beginning of giving love to yourself. Partaking in regular exercise is also just as important. Find what exercise makes you happy and stick with it. If you struggle to find something, look to outdoor activities such as hiking or walking with friends so you are exploring and encouraging a different outlook while doing so. Dancing, surfing, swimming, climbing, playing a sport are all linked to positive energetic expressions. Because that's what the purpose of the sport is, to raise your vibration and keep your body healthy as you release energy. If you don't have a favorite exercise, keep trying! Walking with friends is exercise, and often many towns have free walking groups, so you could also meet someone new whilst getting involved with your local community.

My personal favorite form of exercise is yoga. Yoga is linked to spiritual practices because it is an activity that moves energy through your body in unique ways. As you move your body into different postures you encourage clean air to circulate throughout and essentially you are moving air into areas that rarely receive such a surplus of vibrating energy. And this is why there are so many benefits of yoga, because you are cleaning and replenishing the energy of your organs and muscles and many hidden places inside your body. It's an activity that focuses on harmonizing the flow of energy between your mind, body, and soul. Energy work is how we heal and nurture ourselves.

Have a look at your own exercise routine by answering the following questions in your journal:

What's my favorite exercise?
How many times a week/ month do I exercise?
What's a new activity that I've always wanted to try?
What's stopping me from trying this activity out?
What's the worst outcome from trying this activity?
What's the best outcome from trying this activity?

Partaking in exercise at least one to three times a week is important for your mental and physical health. If you are not doing this already and need support, have a look at your local community and see if there are any activities that you could experiment with.

Healthy Soul

The time has come to let the past go.
Replace that space with something inspiring,
something full of love,
something that complements the person you are becoming.

Mind + Spirituality

To harmonize the energy of our mind, we need to remind ourselves that we have complete control over it. And in order to take control of our mind, we need to understand the way that our mind works. The mind's primary purpose is to solve problems. Give your mind any question and it will automatically list a number of probable options for you. The very first idea is usually your intuition, and then, the mind's rationality takes over, creating various ideas, scenarios, and suggestions. Our mind likes to be analytical while providing endless possibilities for you. As we draw attention to one idea, we can multiply that into countless others, regardless of what is true, just a logical knock-on effect from the way our brain works. Now that we know this, we realize the importance of intercepting our thought process and ensuring that positive questions and suggestions arise when confronted with negative thoughts.

An example of this might be that you are thinking "I am not good enough." Your brain will logically spiral into all the reasons why this statement could be true; such as, "I don't have the right people around me, I'm not pretty enough, my eyes are too close together." And the list goes on. But if we intercept that negative thought quickly with a positive question such as "why do I believe I'm not good enough?" and allow the answer to come through, a new perspective has an opportunity to arise. We continue to ask the question, following the cord to where this belief came from, and from there we challenge it. We find out whether this negative thought belongs to us or someone else. Regardless of where it came from you have the power within you to entertain the thought (let it exist), or to knock it back and let it go. The choice is always yours. Don't give your power away.

"You are not your thoughts" is a common spiritual concept that is recited often. Let's break this down. This statement implies that "you," your true self, is in fact separate to your mind, "your thoughts." And the reason that we can say this is because of the way our brain works without interference.

You = a soul
Your thoughts = the result of your mind/ brain = an organ of your body.

Your mind's natural function works in a survival mechanism. Therefore, it's common to overthink about problems, fears, and sorrow as the brain's organic reaction is to solve and protect us. But life is not a mystery to be solved. It is a moment in time to observe, experience, and explore. In order to create peace it's important to provide our mind with our own answers, our own acceptance of these issues at hand so that we may heal, learn from them, and let them go. You will continue to rethink and overanalyze until you learn how to master your own mind and accept that some things are not going to be figured out. Spiritual practices that help to calm your mind include mindfulness, meditation, practicing gratitude, and accepting things that you can and can't control.

Mindfulness is the act of bringing your awareness to the present moment and observing life around you without judgement. If we clear our mind to neutralize our perception of life as it plays out around us, we discover the secret to creating peace in our lives through self-awareness. For it is through a consistent practice of bringing our attention to the present moment that we are able to remove the troubles of fear, grief, sorrow, hurt, and blame. This is because when we do this, we are recognizing that our feelings and emotions are the result of an attachment to a negative experience, and not the physical result of that event. The more space we can create with thought, the more we are able to observe and choose our thoughts, the easier it becomes to question those thoughts, and to challenge those thoughts. We need to remember that we have power over our thoughts. When we take on the role as the observer of our emotions and feelings with the help of meditation, we are provided with comfort to problematic mental health issues such as depression, anxiety, and stress.

When you meditate, the first thing you do is observe your breath, and this alone is one of the simplest and effective actions to sink into a deep stage of relaxation (refer how to meditate on page 87). Try it with me now. Breathe in and out very slowly. Notice how your body moves gently with every inhalation and exhalation. Bring your awareness to the gradual expansion and retraction of your stomach that you create with each breath. As you focus your attention on this movement you are clearing your thoughts, you are becoming the observer, holding no judgement or pressure to be anything more than just a simple breath in and a simple breath out.

When you combine this exercise of being the observer with mundane chores during the day, you will organically invite in more harmony, peace, and most importantly, more space with your thoughts. The more space you give to your thoughts the easier it becomes to choose the right thoughts for you. Let's look to washing the dishes as an example of bringing mindfulness into ordinary tasks. You could clear your mind, and become the observer to appreciate all the combinations of textures as you wash them. The water, the soap, the object, the drying—become aware of each moment that you are connecting yourself with these energies. You can also look at this process as the actual result of it. Such as, you are purifying these utensils that you eat with. You are witnessing something tangible transform from dirty to clean, dark to light. Use this process while cleaning yourself too; imagine you are the object and as you clean yourself you are clearing your energy also. Lastly, remind yourself that presence is achieved by connecting with that sole object in that moment of time. You and the glass. You and the plate. Notice the texture of the utensil, notice the hardness or softness and the contrast of such an item. By clearing your mind and focusing on the task at hand you are able to clear your thoughts over other areas of your life. You are not there thinking, dwelling over past memories, or feeling anxious for the future. You are there in the moment with no distractions, and nothing around you to take control of your mind. If you are able to enjoy these moments of stillness, it will assist you in learning to be mindful elsewhere in life.

Other daily acts that open an invitation for mindfulness are:

- Watering the plants—connect with the water as it nurtures Mother Earth. Watch as the water runs over the plant and into the soil. Connect with the water and Earth as they mold together.

- Exercising—when you exercise try to focus your attention solely on the activity and the movement you are creating with your body. Use your breath to clear out any stagnant thoughts or negative energy.

- Cooking—focus solely on the task at hand. Be present with each action, each ingredient, give it love and thank it for its gift.

At every moment you are offered an invitation to be at peace, to be the observer and allow life to flow. Accept this invitation by turning to your breath to anchor your presence. But of course, this sounds so easy to understand; we still have more work to do. Let's look in depth at our negative thoughts.

Letting Go of Negative Thoughts

This pain that you feel is not real. You aren't physically being harmed. This pain is the result of an attachment to a thought. And you have the power to choose your thoughts. Holding onto this thought is the same as holding on to stagnant energy: it gets heavier over time. And we can only hold on to a specific amount of energy; therefore, by holding on to this negative thought or past memory, we are not allowing anything else to move into this space. We are literally closing ourselves off from happiness or from something wonderful coming through into our lives, because we are choosing to hold on to negativity.

If we don't remove the dead leaves, the plants will die. Why? Because the energy that the plant absorbs from the sun to feed itself is drained as it tries to keep the dead leaves alive. So, we prune them. We remove the dead weight to allow life to vibrate.

We need to apply the same principles of pruning leaves to our thoughts. Remove those thoughts that weigh you down. Those thoughts are only kept alive from you choosing to feed them. We need to let go and grow. But it's not just about turning our negative thoughts into positive ones, we need to also understand why they are there in the first place. We need to get to the root of the problem and the best way to do this is by probing the questions such as:

Why do I think this way?
What happened in my life to think this way?
Did someone tell me to think this way?
Is this the result of a limiting belief from myself or someone else?
Is this belief true?

We follow a thread from the surface of the problem to the depth of root cause of how, where and why. And from this space, we inject love into it. We heal, forgive, and let go of what we once thought. And slowly, bit by bit, we will change our perception of our life.

By igniting positive changes into your life you will, with repetition and time, learn how to manage your own mind and thought process. The more you step into the position of becoming the observer, by allowing situations and challenges to enter your awareness without judgement, the easier it will be for you to solve any problem from a place of love.

Negative thoughts and past memories can also be viewed as energy that needs to be released, that needs to be transformed into positive vibrations, for when it hovers in our being, we are holding on to that energy and not letting it go. We are holding on to past memories, past pain, traumatic experiences, thoughts, and feelings that are not serving our best interest. Remembering an old version of yourself that you cannot release is not supporting the evolution of your soul's energy. You can mourn that version of yourself, but then set to work and find out who this new person is that you are becoming. We will explore more about this in the chapter on Spiritual Awakening (page 233), but right now, let's look at moving this energy through, releasing it, and replacing it with positive vibrations.

Breathing Exercise to Remove Negative Energy

Imagine a golden sun directly above you and its warm light is shining onto the crown of your head. These rays of light are glowing with brilliance, they nurture your soul and give strength to your body.

Breathe In

"I am safe, I am loved, I am at peace."

Feel the light drip down over you like raindrops on your body as it nurtures you with love and safety.

Breathe Out

"I surrender anything that no longer serves me."

Release any energy that is stuck in your aura and allow the sunlight to transform and replenish this energy.

Breathe In

"I receive healing, nourishing light energy with every breath."

Allow the golden sun to gift you with positive vibrations.

Breathe Out

"I release all of my stress, troubles, and fears that are holding me back from being true to myself."

Let go of any thoughts that are weighing you down for you are always safe, loved, and protected.

Your breath has the power to eliminate any stagnant energy in the seen and unseen realms. Using your breath and visualization, you can release all of the negative vibrations that you are holding on to in your mind and body whether you are consciously aware of it or not.

Understanding Hurt and Pain

It's common to move closer to the side of pain because it's a familiar feeling. We know what it feels like to be disappointed, distressed, and hurt. But we rarely know what it feels like to be loved, to love ourselves, and to trust the Universe. And so, we use experiences that create a feeling that we know so that we can define ourselves. But by doing so we are cowering away from the truth of our being. We're too scared to learn about our own divine internal self, for we are hiding in the shadows and seeking comfort in the darkness. But the time has come to break free from the shackles of your past. Let yourself illuminate. You are worthy of great things. And the beauty of what you can achieve in this lifetime is limitless!

When people point hate at you, remember that it's really the hate within themselves that they are revealing. They aren't willing to shed light on their own sorrow, their own grief to heal and understand why they feel this way. And so, they take the easy option—to shift the blame so they can ignore the truth. Try to meet them with love and understanding. Give them the patience and compassion that they wish they could give themselves. And have faith that in time they will see the truth. It's not your job to fix anyone. No one is born evil. It's the result of pain inherited from their surroundings and those who've passed. People inflict hurt on one another so they don't have to deal with the pain inside of themselves. When they show acts of hate, it's because deep within there's an absence of love. It's not your role to fix them. Your role to play is to be the light, set the standard of the kind of relationships, love, and respect that you deserve. If someone in your life is not honoring your being, you need to be vocal and let them know that it is not okay.

To understand how to heal hurt and pain, let's look at this example:

A trauma has shaken you to your very core. To the point that you don't know how to get out of bed, you don't know how to function. You believe it has happened for a reason, but you are finding it pretty hard to see clearly what that reason is.

Take a deep breath and know that this moment will pass. But first, we need to look at the situation with a different perspective. We need to take a step back from the drama and see the problem from a bird's eye view.

Remember that we are made of vibrating energy. Inside our cells are tiny atoms that move and shake. So think of this pain that you are holding on to as trapped energy. This trapped energy is being held in your body and mind which makes it uncomfortable so it feels like pain. But this pain is just stagnant energy that you are holding on to; it is the result of an emotional reaction you have had to an event in your life.

To simplify this further—something has happened to you, you have reacted with a strong emotion, and then this emotional energy is trapped in your body. You are holding on to it. The actual event didn't cause you pain; it was your emotional reaction and attachment to the event that is causing you pain. It's normal to have an emotional reaction; it's not something that we can control when it happens, but with practice, patience, and understanding, we can learn how to change our perception of the world which in turn is where your emotional reaction stems from. This is what is causing you pain; it's your emotional attachment and reaction to the event.

By holding onto this pain you are causing suffering inside your own mind. This suffering is imaginary, and yet it feels unbelievably real. The emotional turmoil that you are experiencing replicates a physical pain, and in turn, this pain transforms into stress—the leading cause of many serious illnesses. It's important to remove and clear this emotional baggage from your body so that you are able to allow new energy to move into this space.

When we start thinking in terms of energy, our healing becomes clearer. Anything that is unhealed in our body is in the form of blocked energy. We need to focus on moving that energy elsewhere and transmute that energy into new vibrations. Give yourself permission to be an alchemist of the energy that you contain.

How to Heal

1. **Acknowledge the experience**
   Accept your current situation by writing down your story through your journal. Express all your emotions and reactions as you document exactly what happened.

2. **Honor your emotions**
   Now that you have written down your emotions (created a tangible expression of this energy), it's time to honor them. Give yourself permission to grieve, to cry, to shout, to scream. However feels right for you to let the energy go. We want to let the energy be released!

3. **Forgive and send love to yourself**
   You acted the best you knew how to at the time. You need to

forgive yourself, let go of the regret and shame that you carry. Remember that this experience will make you stronger. Promise yourself that you will learn from this mistake. Speak to yourself in the mirror and forgive yourself. Give love to yourself by choosing an act of love that makes you happy. Write yourself a love note or have a beautiful bath to give yourself that love.

4. **Forgive and send love to the person who hurt you**

   If someone did something to cause you pain, remind yourself that they also acted from their level of conscious awareness. It doesn't excuse their behavior, nor did you deserve it. Their actions enabled your soul to evolve and grow and with time, patience, and compassion, you will be in a place of understanding. To release the pain we need to forgive and let go (page 173). This is the only way to move forward.

5. **Meditate to allow the energy to move through you**

   Use the energy healing techniques we explored earlier in the book to identify where this pain is, to release and cleanse it. Imagine beautiful nurturing vibrations coming from Mother Nature below, and the cosmos above. Visualize this energy cleansing your body and mind (page 65).

6. **Spend time with Mother Nature to replenish your energy**

   The simple act of spending time in nature will heal you. Go for a walk, sit in the park, do some gardening. Do something that connects you with the abundance of natural resources around you. Your energy will heal with or without your knowledge. To deepen your practice, remind yourself what each energy represents as you connect with it, say a prayer, or ask for its blessings as you allow its energy to move through you (page 54).

7. **Trust that all is happening for a reason**

   What is to be gained from this experience? Journal through to find comfort within your intuition. There is always positive amidst the darkness, we just need to be patient to allow the light to shine through. Journal through your emotions and self-reflect to help discover the meaning behind the experience. The answers might not come through to you for a long time (even years!). But trust and believe that someday it will become apparent. All you can do is have faith.

8. **Move closer to positive vibrations in your life**

   Find what it is that makes you happy and do it every day. Write lists, fill your week with positive activities (making sure you leave time for fun activities on your own to connect with your soul). Start "doing," get out of your mind, and move that energy. Express yourself and experiment with life.

When we heal ourselves from our past pain, we not only heal ourselves in this life, we also heal the children that come after us. Because, just as we inherit wisdom from our ancestors and our past lives, we inherit the pain that was felt, the lessons and the grief. And this is why it's important to not only heal ourselves for us, but also for our future generations. The process of healing is crucial to the evolution for humanity. We cannot create peace in the world if we do not have peace within ourselves.

Ancestral Healing

Our ancestors faced horrific wars and experienced a time of extreme transitions. As countries were oppressed and colonized, a huge displacement of generations took place, patriarchy commenced, and the repercussions of such behavior is still tormenting us today. Equal rights for gender, race, sexual preference amongst many other urgent matters of attention are still in battle today. And the reason why these problems are unresolved is because there are still deeper truths to be revealed. Many people are blind to the truth, leaders of countries have killed to keep their secrets hidden, and the unnecessary battle against countries for greed and hierarchy is aiding to keep these problems erupting and bleeding. We, as a collective, need to raise our consciousness closer to love so that we may heal our ancestors, and make a safe space for our children, for there is far too much pain, suffering, and hate amongst us.

Our ancestors faced great wars and difficult survivals. It is normal that we inherit the past pain either energetically, or from the misunderstandings of generation gaps. Our role is to feed love into this past pain and focus on how to heal so that we can evolve as one. We have been given a sacred task to face this uncomfortable, yet necessary process of healing so that the hurt, anger, and blame can rest in the past and we can focus on creating a world that we love together in unity. Let us pray and do the hard work so that the children who follow us will never feel the weight of this burden. Healing is necessary for the evolution of consciousness. It is a sacred part of our path to enlightenment.

It's easy to get caught up in our own pain and misery—"My mother is a strict narcissist, my father doesn't love me"—but we forget to learn the reasons why they are the way that they are. We need to apply the same technique of following the thread of one negative thought to the other to reveal where it came from. We need to follow the ancestral line to find out where this negativity originated from. Who instigated evil and hurt first, and why? And how can it be healed? Why do we allow these fears and limiting beliefs to become the truth in our life? Even if you have a difficult relationship with your parents try to remember that your parents did the best they knew how to given their understanding, their awareness, education, and knowledge of the situation. Let's journal over the following questions to discover with whom you have a difficult relationship with.

My relationship with my mother/ father is…
The positives attributes of my relationship with my mother/ father are…
Things I would like to tell my mother/ father…
These are some ways to strengthen the relationship with my mother/ father…
For example, spend more time with your parents (one-on-one time). Tell your parents that you love them and are grateful for their love.

Like all challenges that require healing, the story must be expressed, the truth must be acknowledged, the forgiveness must take place, and a better future must be envisioned and acted upon. There are many elements to connect for such a mass awakening to take place. But the lightworkers are among us, and every person must play their part. We have the ability to heal our ancestral pain, to understand why we are the way that we are. And even if only one person from each family focuses on releasing this trauma, we will together create a better place. But to ignite the change needed in this world, the collective consciousness needs to awaken simultaneously and this requires grave work. But all is not lost, because it just takes one person to ignite change, so why not make that person be you?

There are many practitioners who specialize in this field of work. If you find yourself having a strong calling to learn more about ancestral healing, please find a reputable source who can help, as this work is sacred and deserves expert attention. If this is not an option for you right now, I have included some assistance in exploring this area to help open the gateway and commence your healing journey.

Questions to Heal Our Inherited Ancestral Pain

If you are fortunate to have one or both of your parents still alive, make time to spend with them and ask to hear their story of what it was like living with their own parents (your grandparents). Learn what you can, if they are willing to talk. Some generations are deeply scarred by the difficulties they once faced. Let them know that it is important to you, that it has to do with your own healing journey and that by sharing this will in turn bring you closer. When asking elders to recall uneasy times of their life, finding the right time to ask is as important as the question. When you feel like it is a comfortable time, ask some questions like:

What was life like growing up?
What did you learn from your mother and father (your grandparents)?
Who were you closer with and why?
Were they loving and/or disciplined?
What traits did you carry over (positive or negative)?
What were their biggest challenges and triumphs in their life?

What life event that changed the world did they experience?

How did that change them?

How did that affect your relationship with them?

Do you know much about their parents (your great-grandparents)?

Who were their greatest influences and why?

And apply the same line of questions to their life.

What great life experience did they survive?

When they tell you about the traumatic event, understand what emotions were amplified as a result, and what strength they needed to overcome it. Look over your answers and recognize any patterns of behavior that have been carried over.

What belief system was created as a result of this?

Is this belief system 100% true?

What is the truth?

If we applied an outlook of love to this belief, what would happen?

Would I want this belief for my own children?

A vast majority of older generations lived through the horrors of war, oppression, and genocide. Imagine the pain that someone who witnessed such evil acts would face? Their trust in humanity would be shattered. And from this experience, it is expected for someone to find themselves more reserved and withdrawn from others and from life. This perception of darkness in the world filters down through the generations into the present day. Creating change in the world requires our history to be magnified; our leaders who we trusted need to be held accountable for their wrongful actions. All the darkness that the world has endured needs to be brought out into the light so that true healing may take place. Too many of us are still suffering in silence today. The leap of faith to honor ourselves and our life becomes wider. The beliefs of spiritual philosophy that our connection, unity, and love surpasses all becomes more difficult to comprehend, for there is no justice in the world without equality.

We can heal the world by understanding about the disadvantages created as a result of history's traumatic past and do everything in our power to make the wrongs in this world right. But when we turn to spiritual philosophy and the belief that "everyone is connected," and that "everything happens for a reason," it's hard to stay positive or agree with it. For how is it possible to be accepting and okay of such devilish actions? How do we explain it? Evil behavior is the result of unconscious actions. These souls are not living in their body, they are moving and acting in a different realm of unconsciousness. They act maliciously to make themselves feel alive, to bring their soul through into their reality because they have lost touch with who it is that they really are. They manage to find others who are also in the victimizing state of unconsciousness, of deep darkness, and prey on them too. Hoping to gain some form of insight from feeling hate which is ultimately just an absence of love.

We can help heal each other by creating a safe pathway of love for everyone to walk through together as we listen to the stories of what has been. By learning how others were affected, and how we can help heal will change the future of the world today. The spiritual path is not a journey of pure solitude, for we are all connected and we all need to play our part to weave our future together. When exploring this work we must remind ourselves that we need to be clear in our own connection with our divine self. We need to be living ethically with strong boundaries and strong self-care. It is easy to take over someone else's pain that doesn't belong to you, and with being so close to your own ancestor line, when hearing their pain, we can fall down into darkness too. Always remember that you are the leader of light who is able to clear the pathway for others to walk through.

Holding Space to Help Others

Every challenge that we face, we are experiencing together as a collective. When we help another to heal, we also heal a part of ourselves, and in turn, bring forth peace for future generations. Holding space for others is a spiritual way to assist in the healing process.

Find a safe space for the person who is in pain to be able to express themselves comfortably. Let the unhealed person know that you are holding space for them to express themselves in however way they wish. The person may want to cry or even yell. They may simply want to tell their story. It is in this moment that you, as the holding space healer, are to simply be present with them. Make eye contact and listen without judgement, without needing to give an opinion or trying to fix the problem.

We hold the wisdom to heal ourselves, and when we speak clearly and hear our story out loud in a safe environment we can significantly shift the healing process. When we hold space for someone we are helping them find the wisdom and answers within themselves, and this is done by simply being present. It is a reminder to let them know that they are not alone.

When holding space it is also important to keep your own intentions clear and to not energetically take on the other person's pain, nor open yourself up for your own pain to be triggered. Their story is their journey and yours is yours. Allow yourself to be an open vessel to support the other person as they release and renew themselves.

Ritual to Hold Space

Create a safe environment for your friend to feel comfortable sharing their story. You are supporting their story to be honored and released. There is no judgement, no opinion, nor advice to seek.

Intention:
I am holding space for ... may their story be heard.

Sacred Space:
Fire Energy: I call upon the energy of Fire. May the warmth of your flames release ... story so that it can transform into wisdom.
Earth Energy: I call upon the energy of Earth. May your nurturing vibrations enable a safe, secure, and grounding space for ... story to be heard and acknowledged.
Air Energy: I call upon the energy of Air. May your presence allow a clear communication channel for ... story to be expressed authentically.
Water Energy: I call upon the energy of Water. May your currents soothe our emotions as ... story is shared with confidence.

It may be organic as to how the story will be shared and expressed, or perhaps there is some resistance. Move with the emotions and energy that is expressed. Reassure your friend that you are there for them. State your intention our loud, letting them know that there is no judgement and that this is a safe space.

Action: Storytelling + Creative Outlet
Refer to the following questions to help the story be shared:
Tell me what happened that made you feel this way.

What emotions came through?

How did it make you feel?

What thoughts were circulating?

Do you hold any regret?

Is there something you wish you did or said differently?

If so, act or speak these words now.

How should you/ could you handle the situation now?

What will help you heal?

What wisdom could be learned from this?

How do you want to release this energy? i.e. scream, cry, breathe deeply, dance.

Ask questions that encourage the person sharing their story to take ownership and accept their story to enable the healing process. Once the story has been released, you can look at ways to honor it. Consider creating an activity of drawing or painting together. Reminding your friend of the divine beauty that they hold within and to turn their wound into power.

Closure:

When the holding space session is finished, give gratitude for the authentic and raw voice that your friend was able to give. Give gratitude to the energies and spirits that supported your space. And close the ritual in a way that supports the session. Say an affirmation to support the space being held, such as, "Your story has been heard, shared, and honored."

We can also look to other forms of energy healing to help remove the stress and pain carried over from traumatic experiences in our lives. We can heal our energy through sound such as crystal bowl healing, or touch as used in reiki (a very powerful energy healing technique). We can also look to Shamanism practices which use the medicine of the plant and the energy from the unseen worlds to help clean and remove impure energies from our body.

When making a decision to heal our energy it's important to find trustworthy healers. Research the person and the technique carefully to make sure you are aware of who and what it is that you are inviting into your life.

When we choose to confront the depth of pain within our Spiritual Self, and journey inwards to reveal the solutions that are needed, most often, coincidences will present themselves to us, and the right healers will walk into our life. Healers come in many forms, and often, in unexpected scenarios. It could be through a conversation with a child you meet randomly at the bus stop, or perhaps an elderly woman who you bump into in the grocery store. Sometimes these lucky chances come into your life at the most perfect time and utter a few simple words that help put everything into perspective and help you align with your Higher Self even if it is just for a split second. The synchronicity of such a moment reminds us of the great truth that we are not alone and that our lives are perfectly entwined with each other.

In order to heal this pain and let it go we must enter into it deeply, allow ourselves to feel it, acknowledge and understand where it comes from and why, and then, we can let it go. Think of the pain as trapped energy within your body that needs to be heard and released. Give that pain a voice, allow the emotion to be channeled into something. A healthy way to move through pain is to allow the emotional self to be acknowledged and released. This can be done through a creative outlet such as drawing, painting, writing, singing, or dancing.

Forgiveness

Forgiveness is a strong quality to hold, one that will set you free.

Once we have acknowledged the pain, and are working through our healing process, we can open ourselves up to truly accept our reality through forgiveness. Forgiveness enables us to let go and break free of the past once and for all. When we forgive we allow the emotional attachment to the situation to be released, and for compassion and acceptance to take its place. This can be done through the forgiveness of ourselves, or others, or both. We need to remember that in every situation, everyone is acting according to their own level of awareness. Everyone is doing the best they know how to. We need to forgive ourselves and others for doing what they thought best. When we forgive we are able to truly let go of the experience and move on with our life. If we do not forgive, we hold on to anger, rage, and grief. These emotions trigger stress and eventually lead to illness in our mind and body. Holding onto any form of stagnant energy is detrimental to our wellbeing; it stunts our personal growth and holds us back from living fully and wholeheartedly in the present moment.

But how do we forgive when we are so angry or hurt by another's actions? Try to comprehend why someone would act the way that they would intentionally. Are they battling their own war within their mind? Are they living unconsciously? Were they aware of the impact of their actions and words?

Just because you forgive and accept what happened doesn't mean that you think their behavior was okay. It means that you care more about your inner peace than to let yourself suffer. Forgiveness enables our complete acceptance of the situation which is crucial to our healing journey.

The question is, are you ready to forgive?

When we forgive, we need to forgive ourselves first and then forgive others. Because before we can project our forgiveness onto others, we need to make sure that we are at peace within ourselves first.

Even though it may be the actions of another who caused the initial grief and pain to occur, there is usually a part of ourselves that is disappointed with our own behavior (and this is actually a positive sign that growth of the soul is coming). Perhaps you ignored your intuition, or acted from fear instead of love.

An example of this would be: Your partner has cheated on you, or decided to leave you unexpectedly. Even though you are very angry with him, there is something within that is angry with yourself. Perhaps you are angry that you didn't pick up on the signs, maybe you wish you behaved differently, or even still, maybe you had no clue whatsoever, and you are angry at yourself for that. We need to forgive everything. Forgive yourself for not walking away sooner, forgive yourself for not being stronger, forgive yourself for just not knowing. It's not your fault. You did the best you knew how to at the time. We need to forgive them too. Forgive them for hurting you, forgive them for acting selfishly and irresponsibly. Forgive them for not knowing how to behave. When we forgive we accept what happened and move on to heal the pain that we feel.

Let's go through this in more detail in the following exercises. We're going to explore three journaling exercises to enable forgiveness to ourselves and others. Journaling can be done on its own, or if you wish you can ignite a ritual to support the release and letting go of this pain. The follow ritual can be used for any of the journaling exercises:

Ritual to Forgive

Intention:
This ritual is to support the forgiveness of . . . (self or another).

Opening Your Sacred Space:
Fire Energy: I call upon Fire Energy, come forth and transform my pain into forgiveness so that I may heal and gain wisdom.
Water Energy: I call upon Water Energy, come forth and ease my emotions so that I may release the energy of this pain through forgiving . . .
Earth Energy: I call upon Earth Energy, bring forth great stability as I navigate this space to enable the forgiveness of . . .
Air Energy: I call upon Air Energy, come forth and keep my mind clear as I focus my intention on forgiving . . .

I call upon my ancestors, spirit guides, angelic energies, Grandfather Moon, Grandmother Sun, come forth and assist me in my journey of forgiveness to ...

Action: Journaling + Meditation
In the following pages you will find journaling exercises and meditations to assist with your forgiveness of self or others. Implement them here for your action, and when ready, close the ritual.

Closure:

Give gratitude to the energies that you called upon. If any guidance came through in your meditation or journaling, give thanks to that too. Signal the end of the ritual with a positive affirmation: "I have forgiven ... and I send them love."

Forgiveness of Self—Journaling Exercise

We will be reflecting upon the situation that has erupted in your life to bring forth this great pain. So be sure that you are ready to journey into this.

1. Write down today's date and take three deep breaths to bring yourself into a calming state of presence.

2. Begin your journaling exercise by writing down exactly what happened and how it made you feel. Remember the experience, the words spoken, and the way you handled the situation.

3. Is there something that you wished you had done differently? If you know what actions or words you would have liked to have taken or not taken, write them down. Remind yourself that you acted according to your own level of awareness.

4. Write down the lessons that you learned from this experience.

5. To complete this process, write a letter to yourself explaining how life is going to get better. Write to yourself saying that you forgive yourself.

You need to take ownership for your actions, by honoring and accepting them so that you can release this pain and move on. Be compassionate with yourself as you navigate your experience and reactions. You made a decision in your life with all the resources that you had possible. You did it to the best of your knowledge. And although you made a mistake, you learned from this mistake. Everything that happens in your life is always helping to mold you for the greater good and is part of your unique life journey.

Commend yourself for taking responsibility of your actions and confronting this disappointment and pain, for this is how we are able to grow. Through self-reflection and self-awareness we can change our ways to become better versions of ourselves. Be grateful for this mistake that you have made, for this experience has allowed transformation to take place within you. It was a lesson that helped you step closer to becoming the best version of yourself. By taking responsibility for where we have done wrong we are able to have more control over our actions. Through forgiving yourself, you forgive others.

Forgiving Others Through Journaling

1. Write down today's date and take three deep breaths, grounding your energy into your body.

2. Start your journaling exercise by recalling the person who has caused you pain. Remember their presence and the key situation that caused you this grief. It could be many situations, so take your time and explore through them.

3. Journal through the emotions of what happened and why you feel this way. Write it down in as much detail as you remember it; give your emotions a voice. We need to accept what happened in order to move forward. Accepting, acknowledging, and forgiving does not mean that you approve of their actions, and you don't have to tell the other person that you have forgiven them. Forgiving someone is for your own inner peace. This is how we release the pain.

4. Surrender to the emotions. What can you do to make this situation better? Will forgiveness be enough? Do you also need to remove yourself from the equation, and focus your attention elsewhere once forgiveness has taken place? What do you need to do to heal?

5. Holding on to this pain is only hurting yourself. If you wish that someone had changed their actions, all you can do is change your perception of the matter. See it from their point of view, and make peace with this pain. Why did they act the way that they did? What were they trying to accomplish by doing so? What did they gain from their actions? And what did they lose?

As difficult as this situation can be to move forward from, you need to understand that it is only you who can make this change. It is only you who has the power to forgive and let go so that you can move on. People can only meet you at their level of awareness, you cannot change their perception, only they can. Forgiveness doesn't necessarily change the other person's perception of the matter, but it will change yours. When ready, follow through with the gratitude exercise below to completely let go and forgive.

Sending Gratitude to Complete the Healing Process

1. Begin your journaling exercise by writing down the date and taking three deep breaths. In this exercise we are going to write a letter of gratitude to complete the forgiveness process. This letter is not intended to be sent, it is purely to give your emotions a voice to release the energy.

2. Start the letter by writing the name of the person who you wish to forgive, and then write down the experience exactly as it happened (to the best of your knowledge) and explain how it has affected you. Allow yourself to be raw, honest and truthful. Be completely transparent with your intentions, and say everything that you have ever wanted to. Remember this is never going to be sent nor spoken. It is a way for you to release the thoughts in your head, to release the energy; you can heal through sharing your story.

3. Next, write down the wisdom and lessons that came from this experience. What insight did you gain from this difficult situation? Finding the positive in a bad experience isn't making the experience okay, nor is it dismissing the severity of it, but it is supporting your healing process. It is reminding yourself that we have the strength within to persevere in any situation because we choose to.

4. When you have expressed your emotions and understandings through the letter, give gratitude to the other person, and send them love and light. Wish them well on their journey, send them love, and signal that this is the end of your lesson together.

5. Follow through with a cutting of the energy cord page 200, or release and take back your energy and power page 216.

6. Close your ritual when ready, making sure that you give gratitude to the Universal Energies that surround you. Finish the ritual saying, "I forgive and send love to ..."

Letting Go of the Past

Holding on to the past is like holding on to a heavy weight—it only gets heavier over time. There comes a moment in time when you realize that it's your choice to put that weight down. No one else is asking you to carry it around, you are choosing to. Do you want to feel lighter? If you are holding on to the past, how can you take hold of anything else? How can you pick up something new while you still have your hands full? The time has come to let it go. Today is the day.

When we hold on to past memories, we are holding on to an idea of what was once our reality. But by doing this, we are not accepting the present moment. We are pushing our soul further away from our Spiritual Self, thus losing the connection between what is real and what is not. Our mind continues to drift to a place that doesn't exist anymore, and this serves no purpose. Our soul is not growing by dwelling over the past; we are standing still in time, unable to move forward.

Holding on to past memories is holding on to past energy and this can feel painful. Most often, we romanticize the memory better than it was, because reliving it makes us feel good. But that split second of false joy is causing more harm to ourselves than we realize, for we are ignoring the present moment, and in the present moment is where we find real joy and peace, for this is the truth of our existence. It's scientifically proven that the more we remember a false memory, the more real it will become. Remembering fake past memories can become fuzzy in our brain; there is no line between what really happened and what we think happened. And this is why it's detrimental to hold onto any past memories, especially if they are weighed down with negativity. Because we remember this fake memory as the truth when in fact it is not.

So how do we release such negative emotions? How do we let go of the past? We turn to our rituals, journaling, and meditation.

Ritual to Release the Past

Intention:
This ritual is to release the energy of the past.
I am releasing the energy of …

Opening Your Sacred Space:
Fire Energy: I call upon the energy of Fire, may your flames illuminate this space as I release anything that is holding me back from being true to myself.
Water Energy: I call upon the energy of Water, come forth and nurture my emotions, as I let go of the past that is causing me discomfort and pain.
Earth Energy: I call upon the energy of Earth, come forth and hold me lovingly, as I surrender any fears that are holding me back from releasing this past memory.
Air Energy: I call upon the energy of Air, may your wind soothe my mind, cleanse this space as I release this past memory from my being.

I call upon my Higher Self, Grandfather Sun, Grandmother Moon, my ancestors, spirit guides, and curious spirits who wish to support this ritual of releasing this past memory from my mind.

As you open your sacred space and honor each of the directions, burn some incense, sage, or palo santo to allow the smoke to cleanse the space. You may wish to do this often throughout the practice. If ever you are feeling heavy or that a deep release is taking place, it is time to burn the herbs.

Activity: Journaling Exercise

Turn to a new page of your journal, write down the date and take three deep breaths. Write down the past experience and memory in as much detail as possible. Be as specific as you possibly can. Recall small things such as what you were wearing, what the temperature was, what you ate, and then go into the detail of the incident. The words spoken, the emotions felt. The reactions, and the repercussions of such an event. Write everything down so that the energy can move through you completely.

Have a look at the situation and try to find the positive light. Look for the lesson, look for what was learned. Recite your intention again, reminding yourself that you are letting this memory go completely. If any thoughts or feelings arise from this memory, remind yourself that you have chosen to make peace with it, you have decided to let it go.

Allow any emotions to arise and be released. If you feel the urge to cry, to scream or shout, give yourself permission to do so. You are releasing energy; do whatever you need to best support this energy to be released.

Action: Dance / Movement

Complete the releasing of this past memory with movement. Choose a song to listen to that makes you want to move. Dance your body vigorously to allow the energy to be released from any pain, regret, or sadness that you feel. As you dance and move (do this intuitively), imagine the stagnant energy literally exploding from your body and releasing it out into the world around you. Use your breath to help facilitate this motion. Use every part of your body, shake your arms, your legs—everything! Do this for around 5 - 10 minutes, or for as long as you can handle!

When you finally stop, take note of how you feel as you settle your energy back into your body. You may feel a bit lighter with a buzzing sensation of energy around you. Now that the stagnant energy has been released and it has been cleansed you can invite in new vibrations as you wish. Use your journal to write down what you desire, or close your eyes and envision a new manifestation to take place. You have the power to replace this energy, what energy do you wish to welcome into your life? Refer to the chapter on manifestations on page 264 for guidance.

Closure:
Give gratitude to the Universal Energies and angelic energies that supported your releasing process. You can close the circle by smudging yourself and your energy field one more time. Or by placing your hands on your heart and taking a deep breath in and out and saying out loud, "I have released the energy of... something new will now be birthed in its place."

Confronting Fear

We are only fearful of what we do not know which suggests that fear is a request to learn more information. Have you ever been terrified to do something, only to realize that once you did it, all was okay? The moment you experienced it, you knew what to expect (i.e. had more information), and so the fear diminished. And fear for that particular challenge never resurfaced again. Because your mind knew more about the "fearful" subject at hand. You provided yourself the tools to handle it better.

Fear is a limiting belief. Fear is what's holding you back from being your authentic self. Instead of allowing fear to hinder your path, what if you let fear direct you forward?

Let's put this into an example: I am fearful to apply for this job.
I am scared that I'm not good enough.

But what if you actually got the job? Imagine how wonderful your life might be! What about the fact that just by trying for the job you are building your experience at interviewing, which is a very important skill. We need to learn how to push ourselves to overcome the fear of the unknown by experimenting and trying new things. We need to let our soul breathe so it can grow! When we experiment with choices and activities in our life, we gather experience to become better than we were yesterday. Perhaps the job that you interviewed for wasn't right, but at least you now know. If you didn't try it out, you would never know, and instead you would always spend your time wondering "what if." Wondering "what if" is a waste of your precious time as it steals your relationship with the present moment, thus harming your inner peace. Let's change that "what if" from a negative to a positive, as a stepping stone to take action. "What if I chose to focus my attention on loving myself today? I would feel more fulfilled internally and therefore have more confidence to pursue my dreams."

When we choose to think about something it gives that thought energy and brings more life to its existence. But by not thinking about something, it ceases to exist. If you focus your attention on negative thoughts or fearful ideas, your body will start reacting as though your reality is reflecting this exact thought to be true. Your body will start creating signs of stress and anxious symptoms, which all influence a negative impact on your health. In turn, you may trick yourself into believing that these negative feelings and thoughts are justified, for your body is convulsing in response. Before you realize, you have triggered your own stress and encouraged anxious behavior. All because you chose to focus your attention onto a thought or feeling that represented low vibrational emotions, such as fear, stress, or hatred.

You need to remember how powerful you are. You have the ability to steer your fate. But if you choose to side with fear you will stay small, you will shrink yourself down and hurt your growth. We must always side with love, because in every problem, there is a loving solution, there is an answer that comes from love to be found. The more you choose to find the answers with love, the more natural it will become to navigate this pathway with love.

The next time you feel fear or a negative thought entering your mind, choose to drop it, choose to challenge it, and find the solution that represents love. This is the way forward.

To have fear of our life means we have a lack of control over our mind. We think that we have no control but that's our mind talking, that's not the voice of our soul. To give your power away to the mind is to lose sight of the present moment. When we live consciously in the present moment we are in alignment with the energy of the Universe, thus allowing life to flow effortlessly around us; this is the true pathway to peace and happiness.

Confronting Our Fear—Journal Exercise

Answer the following questions in your journal to help overcome your fears:

What am I fearful of right now?
How can I provide myself with information to combat this fear?
What is the opposite scenario of this fear?
What could I gain from this idea going right?
How can I change this fear to be beneficial to me?
If fear did not exist, what's the best thing that could happen?

Our fear can also be the result of a limiting belief that we have been carrying around with us, either caused by our own experience or even the opinion of another. When you find yourself confronted with a fearful emotion or thought, ask:

Where does this fear come from?
Does this fear belong to me or another?

Continue to challenge the fear by asking more and more questions about why and then prove how love can win the battle. We need to get to the root cause of that lie in order to move forward. We follow the same process as we do with finding the reasons why we hold a negative thought, or hold on to a painful memory or limiting belief. There is an attachment to the negative vibration that we need to reveal to let go and heal.

What is my biggest self-limiting belief?
What is stopping me from fulfilling my true potential?

Try to spin the sentence into a positive light.

I am not very good at . . . but I am willing to learn how to change.
And then continue the sentence further:
I am not very good at . . . but I am willing to learn how to change, and the way I can change is through . . .

Don't linger over your fears, find solutions for them:

I am not good enough—I am enough.
I am unworthy of love—I am love.
I've hurt people—Forgive yourself.
I seek forgiveness—Forgive yourself.

Fear of Making the Wrong Choice

There are no wrong choices in life, there's simply another way forward.

It doesn't matter which choice you make, for it will always be the right one for you in this moment of time. Find peace with each decision by making sure you are trusting yourself and listening to your intuition. Because you are guided by the Universe always. Even if you perceive it as the "wrong" choice, it won't be for very long because something will happen, something will change to push you toward the right one, and most often you will have received a wonderful lesson in exchange.

When we are indecisive of our choices, it means we are ungrounded. When you feel secure in your space and confident in the direction of your pathway, listening to your intuition becomes easier. Practice the intuition strengthening and grounding exercises that we previously explored on page 183. If you are having difficulty hearing your intuition when making big life decisions, try the following ritual:

Ritual to Make Decisions Through Your Intuition

Intention: I am calling upon the energy of the Universe to assist me in deciding between … and …

Sacred Space:
Fire Energy: I call upon the spirits of Fire Energy, please illuminate the pathway so that I may feel my way through to the right decision for me today.

Water Energy: I call upon the spirits of Water Energy, please come forth and soothe my worries as I find the confidence within to make this choice.

Earth Energy: I call upon the spirits of Earth Energy, please keep me grounded as I make the decision to encourage the most rewarding experience for me.

Air Energy: I call upon the spirits of Air Energy, please come forth and bless me with clarity, so that I may see the right decision laid out before me with ease.

Action: Journaling Exercise:

Write down both possibilities and the potential outcomes that will arise from them. What is the best possible outcome and the worst possible outcome? Hover over both ideas and use your intuition to feel the energy of which one makes more sense to you. Go with your first instinct, don't doubt yourself. You have the power within you to make the right answer for you, you don't need to ask anyone else. Just ask the voice of your soul.

Use the energy of your soul to confirm your choice. Place your hand on your heart and rephrase the problem so that the answer is either a yes or no. For example, "is … the right choice for me?" As you state the word yes or no, feel which answer is lighter and which is heavier. The lighter answer will always be the right one.

Meditation to Assist with Making a Decision:

1. Once you have settled into a deeply relaxed and meditative state, imagine you are walking along a pathway and that the pathway then splits into two. On the right is the pathway toward one decision, and on the left is the other decision.

2. Recite in your head or speak out loud as you appoint each pathway to represent each decision in your head three times.

3. Take your time trying to walk down each pathway and be aware of any sensations within your body as you do so. How does it feel to walk down these pathways?

You may find you are unable to walk down one of the paths; you may find that it feels heavy or slow, or sluggish. If both pathways feel easy to walk down, then you will know that either option is going to have its rewards. If neither pathway feels right, allow yourself a few days to reflect over the options. Is there a third pathway you are unaware of? Can you walk down that pathway?

Closing the Ritual:
Repeat the opening of the sacred space in the form of closing, giving gratitude for the presence of Universal Energies. Say your intention as an affirmation such as, "I now know that … is the right choice."

Sometimes when we are unable to make a decision it can also mean that it's not the right time to make that decision. Listen and trust yourself and learn what is right for you. There's no need to ask anyone else, just come home to yourself. Place your hand on your heart and ask your intuition to speak loudly.

Often our fears are hidden within limiting beliefs. And those limiting beliefs are detrimental to us unless we recognize the pattern and learn that it connects to an experience from our life. Do these beliefs belong to you or someone else? To find this out, let's explore your inner child and learn what truth needs to be revealed to assist you in your healing journey.

Healing Your Inner Child

We have all experienced something traumatic in our childhood that shaped our future. It could be something that happened directly to us, or to someone else that we witnessed. Either way, we were affected. And it was at this time that our emotions developed at a faster rate than our logic.

From this experience we developed a limiting belief as a form of a coping mechanism to ensure that the hurt and pain that we felt as a child would never occur to us again. This limiting belief that we developed as a child is then carried through to our adolescence and into our adult life. Psychological studies report that when we encounter a similar situation in our adult life, it triggers that emotional inner child within, and the limiting belief is also triggered, even though this idea is false and goes against all logic. We commonly refer back to what feels familiar as a way of identifying ourselves and handling the situation.

There are three common limiting beliefs connected to our inner child that we see arise repeatedly; these are:

Orphaned Child—the belief that I am all alone
Wounded Child—the belief that I'm seeking someone to save me
Victimized Child—the belief that it's everyone's fault but my own.

Our inner child holds a story of a limiting belief. When we say limiting belief we mean a belief system in place that is holding you back from being your true self. It is limiting you to be able to function properly and view situations with a clear vision with no judgement.

We need to practice healing our inner child by revealing what happened and understanding the truth to discover what it is that is holding us back from moving forward. To heal your inner child you need to identify which one you relate to. We do this by looking at the connected limiting belief system that we have chosen to give ourselves. Let's examine this further.

Do you believe that the world is against you? Or do you think that you are all alone in this world and that a connection with others is unable to ever be achieved because you are too different and no one will ever understand you? If so, you may identify with the Orphaned Inner Child.

Are you constantly looking for outside help to save you? Do you rely on the support of others to soothe your troubles or to provide you with the solutions to your life problems? If so, you may identify with the Wounded Inner Child.

Do you blame your parents, siblings, or outside forces for things that have gone wrong or for things that are going wrong in your life? If so, you may connect mostly with the Victimized Inner Child.

You may connect with all three on some level, and that's normal too. We need to identify the problem before we can fix it. We can't control the life we were born into, the actions of others, but we can control our reactions and the way we handle the problems that come our way. When we blame others, we give our power away. When we look outside of ourselves for answers, we give our power away. We need to take that power back and praise how mighty and strong we really are. The moment we choose to understand, forgive, and take control of the situation, we are able to release the negative energy that is stagnant to our relationship with ourself. The moment we accept our life as our sole responsibility we take our power back.

Sometimes our inner child falls heavily on our line of ancestral lineage, and it can be a direct knock-on effect from our parents. We can inherit their limiting belief system and take them on as our own. Let's explore how we can release these limiting beliefs with the following spiritual ritual to heal your inner child.

Ritual to Heal Your Inner Child

Intention:
This ritual is to heal my inner child, so that I can release any limiting beliefs or negative thoughts that are holding me back from being my authentic self.

Sacred Space:
Fire Energy: I call upon the energy of Fire, come forth and shine your light as you support me on my quest to heal my inner child.
Water Energy: I call upon the energy of Water, may your movement of fluidity soothe the emotions of my inner child and assist me in my healing journey.
Earth Energy: I call upon the energy of the Earth, please open your heart and create a safe space as I reveal the truth of my inner child.
Air Energy: I call upon the energy of Air, come forth and clear the pathway, as I hold my inner child and heal its pain.

I call upon the ancestors of my bloodline, my Higher Self, spirit guides, Grandfather Sun, and Grandmother Moon. Come forth and guide me on this pathway to allow my inner child to heal.

Action: Journaling and Meditation

Once the ritual has opened, follow through with the journaling exercises and meditation on the following pages. When finished, close the ritual.

Closure: Give gratitude to the energies who accompanied you on your journey. State the intention again but as a mantra: "My inner child is healed."

Journaling to Heal Your Inner Child

1. Reflect over your childhood and recall when something of significance happened in your life that you remember. To help, write down the following age groups and any memories of significance that arise: 1 - 6 years old, 7 - 12 years. 13 - 18 years.

2. Write down the experience of what happened; recall it in as much detail as possible that you can remember, reciting how you felt and the emotions that surfaced.

3. Now write what you learned from that experience at the time. Specifically the reason why you thought the situation occurred and what your perception of the world was at this age.

4. From this, look over the three common types of inner child and see who you relate to. It may take a few questions to fall deeper within to bring the idea to light.
   Orphaned Child—I am all alone
   Wounded Child—I'm seeking someone to save me

Victimized Child—It's everyone's fault but my own

5. After you have recognized which inner child you identify with the most, write down the limiting belief that you adapted that helped you cope. What did you do to protect yourself?

Example:
Your parents got a divorce, because someone was unfaithful. This action then encouraged you to believe that love isn't real. That you are all alone and no one could possibly understand what you're going through. Therefore, you have the belief that you will never find anyone who understands you, from this you believe that you are unworthy of love. The limiting belief here is that you believe you are unworthy of love and all alone, you connect to the Orphaned Child. To prove that this belief of yours is correct, you may even self-sabotage, so that this belief stays true for you in your life.

6. Outline what limiting beliefs you have placed on yourself as a result of this inner child identity. Do you recognize your limiting belief throughout your life repeating or resurfacing? If so, write down where and how.

7. Let's confront this limiting belief and tell it why it is untrue.
   Ask yourself:
   Is this belief 100% true? Am I 100% sure?
   What is the real truth?
   How can I change my belief system to recognize the truth?
   Is there anything I need to do to change this belief system?
   How has this limiting belief affected my life?
   Are there any situations that have arisen where I have reacted to protect this limiting belief, as opposed to the truth?
   How can I handle this situation differently?

What coping mechanism do I do to protect myself?

Are there any areas of my life where I self-sabotage to protect the truth of my limiting belief?

Often, we need to forgive ourselves or others in order to change our beliefs, heal our inner child, and make peace with the past.

8. Is there someone you need to forgive to release this inner child? Write yourself or them a letter, forgiving them. Refer to page 174 to support your forgiveness to self or another.

9. Lastly, let's look at the belief your childhood self came to understand as a result of the situation arising. Can you try to see the perspective of the situation through the eyes of the other people involved? Write down the way they may have been feeling or why they acted this way.

This will help you have compassion and understand that things are not always as they seem and furthermore, help you heal your inner child once and for all.

From this exercise you will have discovered your inner child limiting beliefs and challenged the existence of those limiting beliefs. Reflect over your life and see where your problems arise and if you have acted in a way to protect your inner child with a coping mechanism to deal with life around you. What is that coping mechanism and how can you change it?

Through self-reflection we can view our life with clarity, for we realize that with each lesson learned, wisdom is provided, and if we are able to take that wisdom into our psyche it will help change our perception, thus enabling us to move along our life path with greater courage, strength, and ease.

Meditation to Heal Your Inner Child

1. Get into a comfortable position and begin your meditation.

2. When ready, visualize a younger version of yourself, and depending on what age your inner child was affected to adapt this coping mechanism/ limiting belief, this is the age you want to imagine. If this belief is carried over throughout your teenage years and adolescence, continue to imagine these versions of yourself.

3. Imagine each mini version of yourself standing before you. Slowly go through each version of this inner child and them know the truth of what happened. Remind them that they did the best they knew how to at the time, but that their belief isn't true.

4. Explain the real truth of the situation (what really happened from an adult perspective).

5. Clarify their limiting belief and tell them why it isn't true.

6. Forgive your inner child, and send love to them.

7. Ask your inner child if there are any messages for you.

If you have anything else to tell your inner child, do so; if you are ready to leave, give each of these mini versions of yourself a tight embrace and let them know they are loved. You will exit this meditation with a feeling of tranquility and peace.

Relationship Endings

At some point in our life we are faced with the destruction of a relationship. This relationship could be romantic or platonic. It could be the result of someone doing something wrong to us, or perhaps we have been the instigator of acting wrongfully ourselves.

The actual event that led to the collapse of the relationship is not important, because if it wasn't this particular circumstance, it would have been something else. It is the result of what that catalyst provided, the end of a relationship. But why did it end? Because the relationship was not in alignment with your Higher Self and to leave it would help the evolution of your soul.

After we are able to move through the healing process (refer to how to heal our energy on page 160), we are able to reflect over the relationship from a place of peace and acceptance. From here, we can begin to understand with greater clarity the reasons why it ended so that we can learn what it is that our soul really wants. Take your time and be gentle in your healing, but know that like every challenge, this pain will pass through. Let yourself be the alchemist to transmute this pain into power.

Relationships come into our life to test the connection we have with ourselves. We are facing a mirror of what we need to heal within. And that mirror magnifies our own understanding of ourselves and the world around us. When you finally have the strength to look back upon the relationship ending as a positive experience, you will perhaps see the truth as to why it was not supporting your greater good. Perhaps you were being untruthful to yourself during the relationship; an example of this could be by being with the partner for the wrong reasons (not true love, or knowing that the other person felt more strongly about you than what was reciprocated). Or that you were putting the other person first and in turn not respecting your own boundaries by being with them. You were allowing the needs of the other to take priority. Remember your needs and desires are equally as important as your partner.

When a relationship ends, ask yourself:
Was I being truthful to myself in this relationship?
Was I putting myself first in this relationship?
Were there any boundaries that I didn't honor in this relationship?

There is a reason why this relationship ended and when you have managed to soothe your pain and release the energy, you will be able to understand that reason. First focus on healing, and once you have mastered this, you will be able to learn the real reason why it happened. We need to hold faith, trust in the Universe, and remind ourselves that all will be revealed in accordance to the divine time.

When you feel strong and ready to move on, it's a good idea to cut the energy cord between yourself and this other person. We hold an energy cord with every person that we have ever shared an experience with, whether that is through a conversation, eye contact, or a romantic physical connection. The deeper your connection and experience was, the more strength the energy cord holds. Cutting the energy cord between you and another person can be achieved in several ways; my favorite is through a spiritual ritual with visualization, intention, and using your breath.

When we cut the energy cord between yourself and another it doesn't mean that you will never see this person or think of this person again; instead, it allows a new relationship to form. The old relationship, for whatever reason, wasn't working, and cutting this energy between you two will allow a new relationship to take its place. A relationship that is complementary to the person you are becoming. If you are meant to have a relationship with this other person (friendship or sexual), you will now have a new opportunity to create the right connection once the cutting of the cord is completed.

Ritual to Cut the Energy Cord From a Relationship

Intention: I am cutting the energy cord between me and . . .

Sacred Space:
Fire Energy: I call upon the energy of Fire. Come forth and illuminate the pathway so that I may see clearly the energy cord between myself and . . .
Water Energy: I call upon the energy of Water. May your element of fluidity calm our emotions as we the cut this energy cord between myself and . . .
Earth Energy: I call upon the energy of Earth. Come forth and keep my soul grounded as I navigate this pathway to cutting the energy cord between myself and . . .
Air Energy: I call upon the energy of Air. May your breeze bless this space and enable the healing of our souls as I cut the energy cord between myself and . . .

I call upon the energy of my Higher Self, my ancestors, Grandfather Sun, Grandmother Moon. Come forth and assist me on my journey to cutting the energy cord between myself and . . .

Action: Creative Visualization Meditation

1. Close your eyes and take deep breaths in and out until you are in a meditative state. Once you find yourself deeply relaxed, imagine the person whom you wish to energetically detach from in front of you.

2. Try to envision them clearly—imagine their face, their clothes, their smell, their energy, and the way they make you feel. Next, picture a silver cord that connects you to them. See this cord clearly, spend some time defining it. Where is it connecting the two of you together? Is it a place on your body or your aura?

3. Next, say either out loud or to yourself, in your own words, something that honors your time shared, that gives gratitude for the lessons, and then wish them all the best on their journey. An example of this could be:
"Thank you for your valuable life lesson, thank you for this experience. I forgive you and wish you love and light. I release all of your energy that I have held onto, and take back my own power too. I release you."

4. Imagine a pair of scissors appearing in your hand that you can use to cut this cord. And then, imagine cutting the energy cord with the scissors. It may take a few times; repeat the words and/or the action as often as you like.

5. Use your breath to help assist you by breathing out heavily and noisily as you cut the cord. And when the cord is finally cut, allow the image of the person to fade away. Allow any emotions to arise as necessary, and know that they are being released with the ritual.

Once we have allowed the energy to disconnect, we can focus on healing. You can use the energy healing techniques with the assistance of a professional, or through your own self-discipline of journaling, meditation, and natural resources as we explored on page 160. You can cut the energy cord as often as you like and continue to replenish and cleanse your energy from this situation and person as needed.

Now that the relationship you had has been given the honor and gratitude that it deserves, how can you honor yourself more? What more could you do to bring out the greatest version of yourself?

Remembering who you were is often one of the greatest struggles as you have spent so much time with this person that it's difficult to remember who you were before this person came into your life. But the question isn't about who you were, it's now opening up the question of who it is that you want to become (refer to "Manifesting the Ultimate You" on page 262).

Closing the Ritual:
Repeat the opening of the sacred space in the form of closing, giving gratitude for the presence of Universal Energies. Say out loud, "I have now cut the energy cord between myself and ..."

Healing Without Closure

You didn't waste your time.
Those pieces of yourself were meant for giving.
By shedding layers of your past you are growing into something more
beautiful, wise, and stronger than you've ever been before.

Sometimes relationships (platonic, work, or love) end without reasons why or without providing any form of closure. These relationships are extremely difficult to heal from, as you must find the strength within to let go and forgive without answers. Know that healing without closure is always possible, and because the grief you feel is far greater, you will become even stronger than you thought you could. The harder the challenge is to overcome, the more profound the opportunity of wisdom will be to receive.

When faced with such heartbreak, remind yourself that you are divinely loved and guided at all times. Remind yourself that the decision for you not to have clarity or answers over the break-up was requested in your Soul Contract. When moving through the healing process, treat it the same as you would if you had the answers. Trust that it is for your greater good. Journey within to speak to your soul and hear the strength that will support your growth. Accept your current situation and be patient with yourself as you navigate this new life path that is laid out before you.

The first step to healing is to acknowledge the situation. It's very difficult to accept your current life path when the lack of closure is leaving a question mark. Is it over, or isn't it? Is there something greater to be revealed? If you feel there are questions that need answers and your heart is asking for those answers, trust yourself and your intuition to receive those answers. You are worthy of knowing what is true, you deserve the respect that you give. But sometimes, some people are not willing to provide the closure for you; they may not know the reasons why themselves, or perhaps they anticipate that their actions or words will cause more pain and hurt even though an honest conversation has the power to be more beneficial.

Turn to your journal to reveal any insight you may be holding on to regarding the ending of this relationship. Ask questions directly to your intuition to find the truth. Write the questions without holding on to any preconceived ideas or assumptions.

Why did this relationship end?
Was there anything I should have done differently?
What did I learn from this relationship?
What boundary could be created from this experience?

Follow through with forgiving yourself and forgiving the other person as found on page 172.

Heal the pain you feel with the spiritual techniques explained on page 160.

When relationships end there are often physical objects that we want to keep but they remind us of the other person and so it becomes difficult to use them without thinking of the memory that it provides. You may have some items that could be of value, or that bring you joy that you don't really want to throw away, but using them has become too painful. Just because the relationship ended it doesn't mean that you need to dispose of these objects. Here is a ritual to cleanse the energy of the object so that it can hold new vibrations for the new you.

Ritual to Cleanse the Energy From Physical Items

Move through your entire house to remove anything that doesn't align with the new you. Donate or give away as much as possible, and then put together the objects that you wish to keep that remind you of this ex-partner. If you can, bring them together near your sacred space if they are small; if not, it's okay, you can go to them once you open the circle. Put some relaxing meditative music on, as this ritual may take a few hours, depending on how many items you have.

Intention: I am cleansing the energy from . . . (state the item) and I invite in new vibrations.

Sacred Space:
Fire Energy: I call upon Fire Energy, come forth and transform any stagnant energy from this ... so that new vibrations may take its place.
Water Energy: I call upon Water Energy, come forth and nurture my emotions as I recall the memories of what this ... once provided.
Earth Energy: I call upon Earth Energy, ground my soul into my body as I cleanse this . . . from any energy that is no longer needed.
Air Energy: I call upon Air Energy, I allow the power of your presence to cleanse this . . . so that new energy can take over.

I call upon my Higher Self, Grandfather Sun, Grandmother Moon, ancestors and spirit guides. Come forth and grace me with your presence as we cleanse these objects from the energy of ...

Take a few deep breaths and clear your mind, asking for guidance from above. Go through each object individually, and do the following:

Action: Energy Healing

Feel the Energy:
Place your hand over the item and allow any feelings or emotions to arise. In this moment, you can relive memories that you feel are attached to that particular object. Let it play out. But when ready, move through to cleansing and recharging.

Cleanse the Energy:
Cleanse the energy of the object using visualization by first sensing where in the object requires to be cleansed. Use the same process of how to identify the energy that we explored on page 65. Identify the color, texture and density. Once located (it could be the entire object), burn your favorite dried herbs or incense to clear out the stagnant energy that is holding space. Allow the smoke to move around the item and while doing so say your intention out loud again. If you are unable to burn any dried leaves or incense, use your breath and visualization to do so. Envision the energy in the object as a color and imagine blowing the energy out of the object with each breath. Repeat as necessary.

Recharge the Energy:
Now that you are ready to invite in new vibrations, imagine what it would feel like to use this object with clear energy, without the presence of your ex-partner. How would it make you feel? What positive energy will it provide you? Continue to touch the object and envision how you wish to use this item in the future with peaceful, loving vibrations. Imagine a bright light (any color), shining down like lightning from above, recharging the space. Continue to breathe as you allow the energy to be transformed before you. Blow your breath on the object to symbolize the final release. Kiss the item if you feel drawn to as your ritual cleanse and recharge is complete.

Move through the other objects you hold, or if ready, close the ritual by giving gratitude to the Universal Energies that supported you.

Closing the Ritual:

Repeat the opening of the sacred space in the form of closing, giving gratitude for the presence of Universal Energies. Recite the intention as an affirmation: "This … is now cleansed of any past energy."

Sometimes when a relationship ends we worry that we'll never feel the same way about someone again. We convince ourselves that the love we felt was so real and so damn beautiful that it's better to love and feel pain than never to love at all. But when we let go of all these limiting beliefs and recognize that we are worthy of true love, and that we deserve all the things we've been dreaming about, the Universe will deliver it. Only this time—you will feel love in a way that you've never dreamed possible. Your body will vibrate so high you had no idea such incredible vibrations could be reached. So don't give in now. Don't throw away your dream. Don't settle for anything less than what you want. Because everything you want is coming.

A Question of Karma

If we believe that energy never dies and that our soul reincarnates from one life to the next, and that we carry forward the wisdom and knowledge from those previous lives, then running into the same soul from another lifetime is highly probable. Perhaps you have already experienced strange coincidences of recognizing people in this life that you've never met before. Or maybe you have unusual connections with a strong understanding of one another yet it doesn't seem logical.

In the same regard that we have our own personal Soul Contract, we also make promises to other souls to assist in their growth of evolution. We adhere to these promises through karmic debt. These experiences can hold both love and hate in them. These karmic debts can be paid off with one person or many. They can be experienced in the forms, such as in a romantic relationships that doesn't work out, or through dysfunctional relationships with family members, or unfortunately, even violent acts from strangers.

A karmic debt is when you have experienced a past life with someone with whom you acted wrongfully. As a result of that pain you incurred to another, their own profound growth was achieved, and in return, you too received a great lesson, but it may be likely that it is not until the next lifetime. We move through our lives experiencing harsh realities, difficult conversations, and painful endings, wondering why and how could life be so cruel. Yet, we need to remind ourselves that by moving through this pain our soul is able to evolve, for it builds the strength of personal development which is ultimately what we want to achieve in this life. To attain consistent growth we need to open ourselves up to challenges and uncomfortable new beginnings. This is the pathway of our Soul Contract.

Knowing how to face a karmic debt can feel overwhelming. It requires great strength, more so than any other challenge we are faced with, because the depth of emotional ties can be traced back to many lifetimes ago, and to heal a pain that has existed from back then takes serious work. We move through the healing process as we would with any other painful experience, by learning how to acknowledge the pain, heal that energy and release it. But these experiences tend to require therapy or additional help from specialized lightworkers, and if you feel called to get that kind of assistance, do not hesitate; this is what other souls' work is here for, to help the transitioning process.

Clearing out the energy from our past lives may sound traumatic, but remember—it's just energy. We have the power to transform energy, just as every living creature on this Earth does. But accepting and acknowledging your situation is the first step, and in karmic debt, it is the hardest. We don't want to admit defeat, play the victim, or feel sorry for ourselves, but the way we were treated could very much warrant that feeling.

A few memories with certain people or scenarios may have flashed into your mind during these pages, and if so, take note, as that was your soul telling you that these were your own karmic debts to be paid, or they may have already been cleared.

It is possible to clear yourself of karmic debt. At some point in your own evolution of existence, you may have completely cleared yourself from previous attachments with souls, allowing new connections to take place. Just because your karmic debt with someone has been completed it doesn't mean you have reached your final stage of evolution, because there is no final stage. It just means that you have learned all that you can from one another and the time has come to meet someone new who will challenge you, and encourage profound growth within.

Identifying a karmic debt relationship can be done in a few different ways. You could have the sense of knowing, and therefore just asking your intuition if it is true is enough. Use journaling and meditation in assisting you on your quest. Another way is through a past life regression hypnosis. This is best done with the help of an experienced guide and can also be achieved through meditation. Once you are comfortable with meditation and have a strong practice in place, you can attempt your own past life meditation.

Ritual to Reveal Your Karmic Debt

Intention:
I am journeying to a past life to learn about my karmic debt with (say the name of the person whom you wish to learn about).

Sacred Space:
Fire Energy: I call upon the energy of Fire, come forth and encircle me with your love, so that I may journey safely to the unseen worlds and learn what I need to know about my karmic debt with . . .
Water Energy: I call upon the energy of Water, may your flowing currents soothe my emotions as I navigate this sacred space and learn about my karmic debt with …
Earth Energy: I call upon the energy of Earth, great Mother Nature, my love. Come forth and hold me lovingly as I journey to a past life and learn about my karmic debt with …

Air Energy: I call upon the energy of Air, may your cool breeze raise my wings high as I travel to this past life to learn about my karmic debt with ...

I call upon Grandfather Sun, Grandmother Moon, any ancestors, angelic energies, or spirit guides who may help me on my journey to discover the karmic debt between myself and ...

Action: Past Life Meditation

1. Repeat the intention three to five times as you close your eyes and lie down in a meditative state.

2. Breathe deeply five times and imagine a golden pyramid of white light protecting you, and say this out loud: "I am completely protected as I enter this past life to learn about my karmic debt with . . ."

3. When you feel yourself in a deep relaxed state, imagine that you are standing on top of a hill. Envision an opening in the ground with a long stairwell going down inside the hill. Take your time to clearly define the stairwell.

4. State your intention again: "I am journeying to a past life to learn about my karmic debt with (say the name of the person whom you wish to learn about)."

5. Begin walking down the stairwell slowly. At the bottom of the stairwell you are going to find yourself facing a door that will be the entry point into your past life with your chosen person.

6. As you reach the bottom of the stairwell define the door in front of you. Take note of the material of the door, the handle, the frame, and size. Recite your intention again and as you open the door, allow a bright light to overtake your vision and then wait for the light to disperse. Here, you will be confronted with your past life.

When faced with your past life the person may not look the same as what you see in this life. You may be in a lifetime from hundreds or even thousands of years ago. Take your time exploring your space around you. Try to gather information about what country and year it is based on your clothes. A good way to do this is to look down at your feet. We can be different genders, different races, different social classes in past lives. If you need to know something, just ask yourself and trust the answer. If you are lost or stuck, ask to be shown where you need to go; recite your intention again. If you feel fear envision the golden pyramid around you again and remind yourself that you are divinely protected. There is no energy coming in or going out.

When faced with the person whom you had a karmic debt with, ask what happened between the two of you. What role did you play, what life lesson was achieved from this. It may become clear why your roles in this life are intertwined and why one person did harm to the other. Or it may be more complicated and a story has been revealed in front of you that you need to learn in depth what it means. Take your time and come back to this meditation again when ready to learn more about your connection.

When you do realize the truth of your past life together, you can change the situation to heal it. If you did wrong, apologize and send them love. If the other person did wrong, tell them that you forgive them and send them love. Make the situation to be at peace between you two. Make this wrong a right in your past life and allow that energy to transmute through into this lifetime.

7. When you are ready to exit the past life create a door before you, and walk back up the stairs.

8. Recite out loud, "I am coming back into my body of this present life of … (and say your own name). I release all my past lives from my journey and I take back the role of …(your own name)." Say it a few times out loud.

9. Wriggle your toes and hands as you ground yourself in your body once more. Remind yourself that you are safe and that you have left all past lives behind and that you are empowered to be alive in this life.

10. Write down the experience of what happened. In this space you may find greater revelations to be presented before you. Trust these as part of your journey.

Closing the Ritual:
When you are ready to close the ritual, give gratitude to the Universal Energies and any angelic energies that supported your journey. Recite your intention as an affirmation: "Thank you for the wisdom, I have now healed my karmic debt with …"

Karmic Debt of a Twin Flame Relationship

There are conflicting beliefs when it comes to defining twin flame and soul mate relationships. I personally believe that a twin flame is a romantic relationship with whom you have shared a past life with and owe a karmic debt to. A soul mate is a soul whom you choose to meet up with from your past lives to continue to share a soul nourishing relationship with deep, unconditional love and mutual respect. Some people believe in many soul mates, such as friends and family members, and others believe that the role I have explained of the twin flame versus soul mate are actually reversed. To argue over who is right is on the same grounds of which religion is correct. There is no answer, so just trust whatever you believe in your heart.

Sometimes we fall in love with the wrong person. Our intuition tells us to go forth fearlessly and to dive deep into a relationship with someone who we believe to have good intentions. We don't realize that our intuition can also lead us to heartbreak too, but why? Because our soul is striving to achieve transformation, and we need to experience difficult relationships and challenging environments in order to expand, change, and evolve. So if you have walked into a relationship that you believed was going to be a soul mate reunion, only to be discarded in the worst possible way, dig deep within and ask yourself if this was a karmic debt from a past life that needed to be repaid. Karmic debt is not an excuse for unethical behavior, but it can be used to provide peace and understanding for some actions which may be completely unexplainable. Regardless of whether the relationship was karmic related or not, one thing is certain: the current relationship was insulting your soul and it needed to end.

Sometimes, the actual event that leads up to the end is devastatingly traumatic, but it needed to be because the connection you held together was so incredibly strong you needed a point of no return.

Trust that you are divinely guided by the hand of your Higher Self, and remind yourself to journey back within to find the answers you seek. Go through the process of healing from this relationship as we would with every healing (page 160).

1) Acknowledge the pain, give the energy a creative channel to be expressed, move through with cleansing, replenishing, and honoring your internal soul. Take your time and repeat these steps as often as needed.

2) Forgive yourself, the other person, let go and make peace with what has happened (page 174).

3) Follow through with cutting the energy cord, cleansing the energy of any objects, and if you feel capable of journeying on your own to explore the past life karmic debt, do so. Or, seek outside help for assistance (page 201).

4) Once you feel as though you have honored and grieved the relationship and are ready, manifest your greatest self, and the kind of love you wish to invite in (page 264).

Karmic debt does not require constant attention or connection. It requires you to acknowledge the lesson, and open yourself up to grow into a new person. To reveal the truth of your karmic ties refer to the Past Life Meditation on page 210.

When ready, try the following ritual to take back your power.

Ritual to Take Back Your Power

Intention:
I release any energy that does not belong to me, and I take back all of my energy that I have given away.

Sacred Space:
Fire Energy: I call upon the energy of Fire, come forth and illuminate the path so that I may call back any energy that I have given away.
Water Energy: I call upon the energy of Water, may your nurturing love soothe my emotions as I release any energy that does not belong to me.
Earth Energy: I call upon the energy of Earth, bless this space with your healing love as I take back all the energy that belongs to me.
Air Energy: I call upon the energy of Air, come forth and cleanse my aura as I release any energy that does not belong to me.

Action: Breathing and Visualization Exercise
1. Take deep breaths as you visualize the person in front of you whose energy you wish to release from your being.

2. Place more emphasis on the exhalation as you thoroughly let go and surrender any energy that is weighing you back. Imagine their energy being returned back to them.

3. Take another deep exhalation and release any energy that does not belong to you. It doesn't have to be from this particular person, it could be from anyone.

4. State your intention out loud again: I release any energy that does not belong to me, and I take back all of my energy that I have given away.

5. Focus now on deep inhalations. Visualize your own energy being called back to you, either from this person or the entire Universe. Call back your energy through saying your intention once more and imagine that with each inhalation you are bringing life back into your presence.

Closing the Ritual:

Repeat the opening of the sacred space in the form of closing, giving gratitude and thanks for the presence of Universal Energies. State your intention as an affirmation: "I have released all energy that doesn't belong to me and I have taken back all the energy that I gave away."

A personal story of karmic debt

My revelation of karmic debt came through in a strange way. I experimented with different modalities of spirituality throughout my adolescence and adult life, always interested to try out recommendations from friends or like-minded beings who crossed my path. In my early 20s I decided to have a session with a past life regression therapist. The intention for my journey was to see what I needed to know for this life. As a series of past lives came through to me into my visions, there was one in particular that held great weight. When reviewing a past life sometimes you can see someone from your current life in it. But at the time I was quite young and didn't recognize anyone. The story of my past life was that I was a male who had seduced the widowed wife of my late brother. This was seen as a betrayal in my father's kingdom and the punishment was for the woman to be beheaded, but I myself was only to be banished. The feelings, visions and energy played out so vividly, more so than any other memory. I awoke from this past life (after healing the energy of this distress), and continued to go about my usual routine for many years unaware of how this past life may affect me. I had forgotten about it completely until I had met another in my current life. The ending of our relationship at the time was traumatic for me, and it erupted a dark night of the soul which instigated a Spiritual Awakening. My attempt to seek peace in this situation was almost impossible at the time, for the series of events that led me to this relationship was supernatural. My intuition guided me toward the pain, and this in itself was difficult for me to comprehend. I had thought my intuition would guide me to safety, that my intuition (the voice of my Higher Self) would look after me, yet here I was walking directly into heartache. I was unaware that I was about to learn the greatest life lesson, that darkness in itself would also be a gift. My healing journey lasted a few years as I was unable to pull myself out of a deep depression and anger at the Universe for leading me toward the greatest destruction and shattering of my ego that I had ever experienced. I didn't want to let go of who I was. And so my struggle and wrestle with myself lasted a long time. But the moment that I could finally let go and move on with my life was when a flash of that past life regression session I had taken almost 10 years prior came through to me. The eyes of the widowed wife were the eyes of this man who had broken my heart. And just like that, my karmic debt had been repaid once and for all.

Grief and Loss of a Loved One

Death is the natural progression of life in our reality. Although we cannot see our loved ones in the physical form anymore, energy never dies, and their energy is with you always. Death brings forth the gift of impermanence and only from this experience are we reminded to hold life with respect, value, and love.

Although we know that death is a part of the natural cycle of life, we can never really be prepared for the grieving loss of a loved one. We rarely know how it may change us, how it might affect us until we are faced with it. Everyone grieves differently, and there is no wrong way to do so; everyone is entitled to their own process. We cannot place any judgement on another's journey through grief, all we can do is hold space and let them know that they are supported.

Knowing what to say to someone who is going through grief is difficult. Simply let them know that you are thinking of them, that you are sending them healing love and let them know you are there if they need. Don't expect a reply; they are moving through their own grief, trying to learn how to heal, which is a very personal journey.

When entering the stage of grief, we follow the same process as any healing—acceptance, acknowledgement and releasing the energy of grief, sadness, and pain. We give great honor to the time we shared with that person and carry their energy with us in our heart. And with time, we learn how to transform our sadness over their displacement into gratitude for the memories that we were lucky to have shared.

From the early Egyptian civilization we learn about their great respect for death due to their beliefs of an afterlife (reincarnation), for they adorn the body with jewels and gold to carry over into their next life. The idea of afterlife has been present through the ages, and only when Christianity was created did the idea of an afterlife disappear. Regardless of religious beliefs, what we do know on a scientific basis is that energy never dies. The air we breathe is recirculated back into the atmosphere and it is in a constant cycle with ourselves. The water that covers the Earth is the same as it has been from two billion years ago, and this water is regenerated and revived.

So, if we know that death is a cycle of life, why is it so hard to accept? Because of the way many of us were raised we grew up fearing death and believing it was a bad thing. But it is the natural cycle of life. Death is a celebration of our life experience.

Sometimes, when faced with the loss of a loved one, we are grieving over the loss of time that is now unable to be shared with that person. This can be narrowed down further to grieving over the attachment of a particular energy in our life. It's important for us to grieve; these emotions are what changes our perception of life and in turn encourages the evolution of our soul. To feel these rare emotions and love another life is an incredibly profound experience that not everyone is able to share.

Energy in the unconscious world has the ability to be everywhere and anywhere at once. There is no barrier stopping the connection between you and a loved one just because the physical body is no longer present in your life. That energy is still alive near you and around you, if you wish for it to be. The love and support another gives you is never-ending, so for this reason, it's important to support our loved ones to pass over, and remind yourself that you can call upon them for strength at any time that you need. Our loved ones need to pass over so that they may continue to fulfill the evolution of their soul. Just because you cannot see them, it doesn't mean that they are no longer with you. They are still with you, supporting you and guiding you with love. It's just that now, they are supporting you in another form, a different way than before. Their energy is still very alive and present.

Our loved ones who pass over to the other side talk to us through signs and messages when we are awake and while we dream. I connect with my loved ones who have passed in many ways. I call upon them for their blessing and support as I would my Higher Self. Or in the same manner that many call upon God, I speak to them too; I tell them how I feel, what I'm thinking, and this keeps them alive with me.

Sometimes I get frustrated or upset that you're not around. Angry at the world. Angry at myself for choosing this path. But then I remind myself of the truth—this is the path I chose. We both chose to play this difficult role in our lives together. You chose to leave before your time, as written in your Soul Contract. And I chose to grow up without you. We both chose difficult paths in life. But every time I start to wallow in the misery of being alone, I think about you. And the sacrifice you gave for leaving too soon from this Earth. Your sacrifice helped so many people around you. You helped those who loved you to live their life with more meaning, more value, more passion. You reminded us of how important and limited our time is here on Earth. You selflessly gifted us this lesson. And so, on those times that I miss you on my birthday, those times I wish you saw me graduate from school, or could meet my loving partner, or tell me you are proud of what I've done. I remember that you are with me and I thank you for helping me mature a bit quicker and grow up a bit faster so that I could bring forth my unique perspective into the world. Growing up a little faster than those around me has helped me accomplish great things because I know you are by my side watching over me; I know I have my own guardian angel helping me become the best version of myself, helping me utilize the opportunities that are coming my way. I'm not only doing good for me, I'm doing it for us, I'm doing it to make you proud because I know you see me, I know you are with me every step of the way. And I thank you. I love you. You are in my heart always. I feel you every day, in everything that I do. I love you.

Ritual to Connect With a Loved One Who Has Passed

Intention:
"I call upon the energy presence of . . . to meet me."

Sacred Space:
Fire Energy: I call upon the energy of Fire. Beautiful light energy of abundance, come forth and shine the pathway to bring me to ...

Water Energy: I call upon the energy of Water. May your gentle waves soothe my emotions as I connect with ...

Earth Energy: I call upon the energy of the Earth. Nurturing Mother, keep me grounded as I walk to the unseen realms to connect with ...

Air Energy: I call upon the energy of Air. Come forth and bless this space with your lightness of being. Bring me clarity as I connect with ...

Action: Meditation
1. Before going into your meditation imagine a safe space that you can meet your loved one who has passed over. An idea could be a park bench in a garden, a rock at your favorite beach. Maybe you remember their house clearly or somewhere you used to meet all the time. Tell them to meet you there. Call out to their energy,

speak your intention again and say, "I call upon the energy presence of . . . to meet me ..."

2. As you state your intention imagine what they look like, how they feel, the energy that they bring. Allow any emotions to arise to the surface while doing so.

3. Now begin your meditation. Focus on using your breath to calm yourself down for the first 5 - 10 minutes. If you have any routine meditative practices do these first, and then when ready, begin your creative visualization journey. State your intention again and then imagine the space that you chose where you wish to meet your loved one who has passed.

4. As you begin to imagine the safe space, your loved one may have already arrived. If not, continue to focus on defining the space. Go into detail with each element around you, such as the ground or the sky, and define its textures and colors. When you become comfortable in your space, call out to your loved one by repeating your intention again. Ask them to come forth and have faith that they have appeared. Trust your intuition that whatever you feel or see is right for you. They may appear as you remembered them in the physical world, or they may be an entirely different vision to what you are used to.

5. When you have a clear visual of them, or feel their energy near you, ask the questions or guidance you wish to receive. Do you have questions for them? Do you wish to send them love? Do they have any messages for you? You may not receive answers immediately but, if you do, open yourself to receiving them.

6. When you are ready to leave, give gratitude for their time and for their unconditional love. Open your eyes.

Closing the Ritual:

Repeat the opening of the sacred space in the form of closing, giving gratitude and thanks for the presence of Universal Energies. Speak to your loved one who passed and thank them for their presence and wisdom.

Now from this point on, you have established a connection together. Whether you received the messages in the creative visualization meditation you just did or not is irrelevant, for the signs can also come through in other ways, such as through animals, conversations with strangers, music, or numbers.

We can also meet with our loved ones in our dreams. All you need to do is simply ask. Before you go to sleep, call upon them and ask to be visited. Ask to connect, ask for wisdom and advice. Hold faith that they will visit you but don't get caught up in the idea if they don't. Be at peace knowing if they are meant to visit, they will.

You can also journal to them in the same way that you journal with your Higher Self, through your intuition. Once you have envisioned the loved one, write a question and allow the answer to come through without thinking.

My late grandmother visited me in a dream one night when I asked the question, where should I move to? I was at a stage in my life where my soul longed for foreign countries, but I was lost with the direction of where to go. I asked the question during the day, unaware that it would be answered that night. I had a very strong connection with my late grandmother. She is the ancestor whom I call upon with every ritual, and at any point that I need more strength in my life. Whenever she visits me in my dreams she is always laughing with beautiful, loving energy, and I run to embrace her, crying as I tell her how much I miss her as she continues to giggle. I never make note in the dream that I am dreaming and that she has passed, it's just that we haven't seen each other in a long time. That particular night we took a ride on a rollercoaster where she told me that I needed to move to London. When I awoke from the dream I booked my flight, applied for my visa, and moved over shortly after. I had a feeling from the dream that the rollercoaster would represent the wild ride of life, and it has not been short to disappoint!

Interpreting Signs and Symbols

If our reality is a holographic reflection of our unconsciousness, and our unconsciousness is connected to the entire unseen worlds, where all energy "exists," then it is not only possible but highly likely that we receive messages through symbols, animals, and other people around us through the command of our Higher Self, angelic energies, spirit guides, and our loved ones who have passed. You may already believe in this due to uncanny coincidences that have occurred in your life, that are just too unbelievable to be true.

You are always guided and protected by angelic energies in the unseen worlds, and these angelic entities are supporting your growth during this Earthly experience. They are aware that you are facing difficult challenges and they know when you need that sign of encouragement to help you move along. The signs are always presented before you, but sometimes we are so closed off to the belief of hope and faith that we are ignoring them.

Anything that you come across in your life that you question "could it be a sign?" is a sign! But what that sign means, is up to you. Ask yourself:

What do I need a sign for today?
What encouragement do I need to be told from the unseen worlds?
What advice would make me feel better, more secure, more confident in myself and my life choices?

And let your intuition guide you through to the answers.

If you are unsure what that sign means, try to remember what your thought was before the moment happened. The moment before you wanted a sign. Is it connected?

A strong sign from the unseen worlds can be found in Animal Energy. Animal Energy combines any creature alive such as (but not limited to) insects, mammals, reptiles, birds, etc. Animal Energy, including any moving life that crosses your path, is usually a sign from your angelic protectors. This doesn't mean you need to go searching, it has to be organic. Because animals cross our path everywhere, we just don't see them. So, if by chance your awareness is brought to the attention of a moving creature at that particular moment, open yourself up to recognize that it is a sign.

Interpreting Animal Spirit Energy has been explored in depth across Indigenous tribes around the world. If you wish to dive deeper into this subject, be sure to consult these practices, but it is possible to apply a modern approach to interpreting Animal Energy on your own. Questions like:

What are the strengths and traits of this creature?
How do they move through their life?
How do they survive?
What is their position of power in the animal kingdom amongst other creatures?
What are they known for?

For example: The grasshopper is unable to jump backwards, it can only go forwards. To see a grasshopper may mean that you are about to leap into the unknown without looking back. A butterfly transforms from a caterpillar; to see one symbolizes great transformation is about to take place or is taking place. To see a fly, we are reminded that flies have the ability to survive in any situation. They move through rubble and rubbish, finding ways to survive because they are persistent. So, if you saw one it could be a reminder to never give up and keep going. A spider weaves a web carefully in perfect symmetry. To see one may remind you to take your time, carefully placing your next move, to sew your own web, or it may be a reminder that you are a part of the grand web of the Universe, and so it could be an invitation to dive deeper within your connections around you. You will know the meaning of the creature that crosses your path; it will be relevant to your current life obstacles and it will inspire the wisdom of what you need to know today. Like all signs from the Universe, we need to trust and believe in ourselves and the voice of our intuition when faced with them.

Signs and symbols also come in the forms of random songs that play on the radio; it can come from unusual conversations with passing strangers. A common question many ask is the symbolism of angel signs in numbers. You can explore numerology to understand the meaning behind numbers if you are interested in this, or simply know that by thinking it is a sign, is your sign.

Bring that power back into yourself, into your intuition, to your Higher Self, and ask what does this sign mean, and trust whatever is spoken, is answered in the truth.

The Meaning of Dreams

For me, my greatest teacher of the seen and unseen realms are my own dreams and meditations. I believe that our soul travels to the unseen worlds while we dream and connects with spiritual energy to provide us with great wisdom, healing vibrations, and nurturing love.

When we sleep we enter a state of unconsciousness and in this space we connect with our Higher Self, other spiritual energies, and Source Energy (the energy that creates the Universe). It's for this reason that after a good night's sleep we not only feel rejuvenated but we also hold complete clarity over any problems that we once suffered from in the waking world. When our soul ventures to the unseen world through our dreams it connects to Source Energy, and molds back into its natural vibration. In this space we heed wisdom from other spirits or our Higher Self and learn more about our Soul Contract, our purpose in life. Our soul needs this energetic reconnection to nourish and nurture, because "living" in reality is exhausting for our soul. We are constantly experiencing different energetic vibrations of all frequencies, a direct result of interacting with soul energies who are evolving at different times, as well as interactions and situations that arise as a result of learning how to navigate our life path. This is why we cannot live without sleeping; we need to connect back to Source Energy to replenish and balance our own vibrational frequency, or we won't survive. This is why we always feel so much better after a restful sleep, why we are able to make better decisions upon difficult matters, or perhaps even arguments with others don't seem to be as problematic as once thought. While we dream we connect with our ancestors, we connect with other spirit masters, and teachers who provide us with guidance and wisdom.

How to Seek Wisdom Through Your Dreams

Learning wisdom while dreaming is not uncommon. There are many stories of famous inventors, writers, and artists who have dreamed about their creation and recreated it in reality, bringing change to humanity. It's possible for you to also seek advice, wisdom, or answers in your dreams. To practice this, you need to prepare the following:

1) Keep a journal next to your bed and try to go to sleep at the same time every night. Immediately upon waking write down anything that you remember (regardless of how insignificant you think it is). The more you practice the better the habit will become and the more vivid your dreams will be.

2) When you have begun to see a pattern of remembering, before sleeping, write down the question you wish answered and ask it out loud. Think about it before you go to sleep and the kind of guidance or advice that you need. Then tell yourself that it will happen, such as, "I am going to learn how to . . . in my dream tonight. I will wake up and remember this wisdom."

3) When you do wake up, write down whatever you remember (such as colors, shapes, or figures). Then write down next to each "memory" what it means to you. If it doesn't mean anything, write down the feeling it brings, what that item does, or what it provides.

This is how we interpret dream symbols and patterns—through our own unique lens. Only you can do this, no one else. Because the messages you are sent through spiritual signs in reality can only be understood by you. This is because we all have a different view of what everything means. Remember to trust your intuition and go with your first instinct. If you second guess yourself, that's your mind taking over. Always go with your first instinct.

I am also open to believing that perhaps we live in other realities while we dream. This happened to me often when I was younger and I would wake up feeling exhausted! My memory of the dream was so lifelike and I had a feeling that I was helping another in my dream as sometimes it felt as though I had taken their pain with me as I woke up.

The last idea of dreams that I want to bring forth is the potential of envisioning future occurrences in your reality through dreams. Often what we call "déjà vu," the feeling of experiencing this moment prior to it actually existing, can often be through a dream you may have had. I have personally experienced this many times, waking up from dreaming and remembering my dream vividly. Who was there, what we said, what we did. Only to then live out that dream in my waking life a few days, a few months or even years later. And knowing what was going to happen because I had dreamed it. Often these moments are a split fraction of a second. Don't think for a second that if you have a bad dream it's going to come true. You have the power of what to invite into your waking life. Don't give that power away. But the reason I want to correlate these two ideas together—déjà vu and dreams—is to encourage you to pay attention to your dreams more often.

Awaken thy Soul

The old you no longer fits. It hasn't for a while now,
but you've been in denial.
Surrender the need to control your life.
Trust in the mystery of new beginnings,
of unwanted changes, of break-ups and break downs.
This is all meant to happen.

You are being asked to walk a different path.
One that is more suited to the person
you've always wanted to become.
But you're scared.
You don't know if over the hill there's magic waiting.
But something deep down inside you is telling you that there is ...

The most miraculous world of love, success, and peace
that you've always dreamed about is waiting for you.
And it's coming to you.

You don't have to do a thing.
Just open your arms and your mind
to embrace the change that is being gifted.
Close your eyes and come into your heart center
as you flow with the harmonic vibrations of the Universe.
This is the way forward.

Spiritual Awakening

At some point in your life your Soul Contract takes charge and a gigantic shift erupts your peace. This shift can be triggered from many circumstances, such as foreign travel or a kundalini yoga session, but it most commonly occurs from a traumatic experience, for trauma has a way of influencing us to become someone we've never been before, forcing us to learn how to live and how to heal in an entirely new way. The positive result of that trauma and gigantic shift of perception is what we refer to as a Spiritual Awakening for it is as though you have just awoken to realize your life and every element in it will never be the same again. Everything that you once believed in, everything that used to make sense to you, has been completely flipped around and nothing is the same as before. You can never go back to the old way of life, the old outlook, the old understanding. You can only move forward. But before the smell of fear enters your mind, take a deep breath, place your hand on your heart, come home to yourself, and remember your strength within. You have the ability to handle anything that comes your way. Why? Because this is all a part of your Soul Contract.

Your soul is asking for you to view the world around you with a new perspective. One that aligns with who it is that you are destined to become. But to enable this change of perspective, to become who you have always wanted to be, your whole world needs to be turned upside down—your understanding of yourself, your loved ones, your home life, maybe even your career. Such a drastic change in our life can create extreme confusion, for how are we meant to know how to solve such a demand, especially if our lives were already flowing in perfect harmony? But even if your life appeared as though everything was fine, there was something at the core level that needed to shift, something that needed to be changed so that the energy of your soul could evolve and transform into true greatness. And for this to take place, you need to unlearn what you thought you knew and relearn the truth of who you really are.

We call this invitation for transformation a Spiritual Awakening because of two reasons:

1. Spiritual—because you are now forced to gain a deeper connection with your soul and your reality to change your perception of life.

2. Awakening—because it is as though you have awoken to a new way of life, a new perspective that you had never thought could be possible before; yet it had always existed, you have just now opened your eyes to see it for what it really is.

But the process of change can feel daunting. Letting go of what you've held close to your heart your whole life to now bring new ideas in can feel overwhelming. There's so much to learn, so much to do. And just that fear of not knowing can overtake our rationality, keeping us amidst the process of transformation for a long time, terrified to move forward.

We often refer to the metaphor for transformation as the caterpillar to butterfly, for such a vast transformation has taken place removing the old way of life completely. We'll use this analogy to understand why it is important for us to lean into the transformation and move forward when faced with challenges.

Think of yourself as the caterpillar who has woven itself to sleep in its cocoon. Except that now you have awoken inside it and you are scared to open up and look outside to see the world. You are so comfortable in your darkness that you don't even realize that you're about to transform into an unbelievably beautiful butterfly. You are holding tightly to the cocoon; it's safe in there. You know what to expect. You've been crawling all your life, and you're happy crawling. You feel secure on the ground. But you don't know how incredible it could be to fly. You have no idea because you've never tried. But instead of giving your wings a chance to spread themselves fully you keep yourself small by resorting to your usual coping mechanism and choosing to side with limiting beliefs, such as:

Maybe you think that no one has ever experienced your journey and so it's not worth your time trying to make the effort to connect with anyone else to find out. You might think something like, "No one understands me, no one could possibly relate to what I've just been through. My whole life has changed! I'm not even going to bother and try to meet anyone because I know I'm right and I'll just feel more alone if I do." (Orphan Inner Child limiting belief #1—you're all alone (page 191). Yet this is the natural cycle of life and the more we share our stories, our challenges and triumphs, the stronger our connection with others will become and the more pleasurable our life will be. For we will be assisting in deepening our understanding of the spiritual philosophy belief that "everything is connected" (page 41).

Or perhaps in your Spiritual Awakening you relate to the Wounded Inner Child, and you stay miserable, scared, and confused, waiting for someone else to save you. The butterfly traps itself into its cocoon waiting for another to show them the way. "I'll just wait here until someone comes to saves me and shows me how to fly." But the truth is—no one is going to save you, because you are perfectly capable of saving yourself. Even if someone did come along and managed to "save" you, it won't be fulfilling because you haven't truly done it for yourself. You are giving your power to another, and you weren't born on this Earth to give your power away. You were born to create the life that you want. And even if you don't know what it is that you want, your Soul Contract does, and your Soul Contract has shifted your world around so that you can achieve your dreams.

The last limiting belief is connected to the Victimizing Inner Child, believing that it's everyone else's fault but your own that you are here. You might be thinking, "Someone should've told me this was going to happen! Why didn't my parents/ siblings/ friends tell me that I was going to change? It's their fault this happened!" And instead of focusing your energy and attention on trying to figure it out for yourself, you focus your attention elsewhere on blaming others; in theory—you're giving your power away. You are ignoring the fact that everything is energy; you are made of energy and you have the power to transform this energy into the greatest success you have ever desired. Everything that you have ever wanted is waiting for you to take it.

When faced with the Spiritual Awakening process we need to take a leap of faith. Break open the darkness of your cocoon that you have rested so peacefully in. Now is the time to show the world your wings, your beauty, your true essence. And when you do, you will fly higher than you ever thought possible! Your vibration will be raised to an entirely new level. This new perspective is going to be the most incredible change in your life! But in order to enable this new perception you have to be willing to look at and change every element of your life so that you can become more aligned with your true self. You will find yourself being drawn to focusing more on your own personal development and you will adapt spiritual practices that will support this growth of your soul.

Your Spiritual Awakening will remind you that you are connected to wholeness, you are always connected to the divine Universe, both the creator and the created. You may have had glimpses of your connections with this truth before but it didn't stick and so you moved your attention back to soft vibrations and distractions. But your Spiritual Awakening is making you open your eyes to the truth in a way that will never allow you to close them again.

Navigating the Spiritual Awakening process may feel intimidating. You may feel at times that you cannot go on, that nothing is working out for you, that everything is going against you. You may feel more inclined to recluse into depressive thoughts or anxious feelings—because at least then you could define what is going on in your life. You may spend a long time searching for answers that never seem to come, and you might be asking for help but it never arrives. This is the darkest part of the Spiritual Awakening process and yet this is still the very beginning, because once you learn what and how to change, you still need to implement these changes to take charge of your life.

The Spiritual Awakening process can be categorized into three stages:

Stage One: A Calling From Within for Change
This is the invitation for transformation and it usually comes as the result of a traumatic event. Depression and anxiety are both mental health challenges that may arise from this experience, and if they do we must focus on healing this energy as we would with any other healing (refer page 160). Stage one is all about learning "what" is happening to you, with a focus on trying to stabilize your emotions and feelings. It's feeling the energy shift within and around you without your control. It's a moment to tune into the emotions overflowing, realigning with your soul and learning how to channel the wisdom from your intuition within.

Stage Two: Relearning Your Inner Journey

You've now healed the trauma, but you are craving a deeper meaning in your life. This stage signifies in-depth self-reflection in your journey of self-discovery. You will spend a lot of time following the seed questions of "who am I?" "what am I doing?" "where am I going?" Although you may have determined conclusions about these questions before, the event prior has enforced you to lose these beliefs. The second stage is a focus on "why" this is happening as you nurture your thirst for knowledge and fulfill your desire for a better life.

Stage Three: Creating the Changes as You Step Into Your Power

By now you have moved through the healing process and are open to learn how to live authentically and step into your power fully. You understand that the wisdom received in exchange for the trauma has shaped you in the most powerful way and you are eager to manifest the vision of your future self clearly while being proactive in taking steps to reach these goals. In the third stage we are looking at "how" we can implement what we have learned consistently. We implement the changes into our life to become the version of ourselves that our soul is craving.

We will explore each stage of the Spiritual Awakening process and learn journaling exercises and rituals to assist in the growth of your personal development journey. Remember to never be upset with yourself for taking a long time, or wanting to move out of one stage into the next as everything is perfectly on time. You may not realize why you aren't going to the next stage even if you feel ready; remember that it's your Soul Contract taking charge of this decision. So just accept where you are right now, surrender your fears, and lean into the challenge. You are taking a gigantic leap down the spiral of your Soul Contract and jumping deeply into the growth of your soul.

Throughout your healing process you need to remind yourself to shift the blame of "why is this happening to me" to "what is this here to teach me?" If the answers aren't coming through to you, have patience and know that the answers will come to you at the right time. We need to become comfortable with the unknown. We need to learn how to live with uncertainty and find peace within ourselves. The more time we spend contemplating over the past or worrying about our future, the more our souls are robbed of the joy of the present moment. If we look to the present moment we find all the answers that we could ever need. We are surrounded with the wisdom of ancient ancestors that have passed on from generation to generation who hold the secrets of the Universe. From them we learn the scientific formula of the creation of life that proves that nothing is by chance, everything is perfectly aligned, and it's because of this particular recipe of heat, water, atoms, and chemicals between the sun and Earth that life here is possible. Our planet could not survive had it been any closer or further away to the sun than it is now. We literally are a living miracle! What an incredible thought knowing that everything aligned perfectly in the Universe to enable life to form, and for you to be conceived. You are not here by accident. You are meant to be living this life! Everything in your world has happened for a reason. And that reason is for you to be here and share your authentic medicine with the world!

Your Spiritual Awakening is the entry point to the greatest transformation you will ever encounter. The beginning will be the most difficult, and you may feel a bit of resistance, denial, and fear. You will know you have reached the middle when you have accepted your situation and are eager to learn how to heal and transition. And when you reach the final stage you will know that you are healing, or have healed, but aren't able to see clearly the reasons why yet. What stage are you at? Accept where you are, get your journal to write some encouraging words about it. For example:

If you are at the beginning:
I feel as though I have begun my Spiritual Awakening process. I am at the beginning and all I see is darkness. I am unsure how to find my way out. But I have faith that there is a way out. I know that this is all happening for a reason, even if I don't understand it right now. This phase in my life will pass, I just need to have patience, take care of myself, and be open to the guidance that will present itself to me.

If you are in the middle:
I have learned to accept that this is part of my story. Although difficult and challenging as it may be, I know that in time I will be grateful for it. I've begun to experiment with new ways of healing, I've started listening to my body, my intuition, and I feel stronger because of it. The sadness is still with me on some days, but I can see that it's my own doing, for I am choosing to bring forth sad memories. I am getting stronger in letting go, to surrender to the unknown and each time that I do I feel myself carried by angelic energy. I know I am not alone and that gives me hope for better days. I trust and believe that I am looked after by the divine Universe at all times. I know that this is a part of my Soul Contract; I just don't know the reason why. All I can do is have faith that all will be revealed when it is meant to.

If you are toward the end:
I have passed the most difficult phase and I feel lighter today. There is still confusion around why this happened, but I know that the answers will come to me when the time is right. I'm enjoying looking after my health in a new way, and I feel the connections around me more intensely. Sometimes they scare me, but then I remember that I am looked after by my Higher Self at all times. I do not worry or fear, because I have been through the worst now. It's only going to get

better from here. I am ready to accept whatever may come my way with an open heart and a curious mind.

This is what it will feel like when you have moved through it:
I see the world and everyone around me for what they truly are. I finally know the reasons why this happened. I am grateful for the experience, as difficult as it was; it has made me so strong, I didn't even know this kind of strength was possible. I didn't know these feelings of connection and love could be so profound. It's as though I am comprehending my existence, and divinity in an entirely new way. There is a new meaning to unconditional love, there is a new meaning to surrendering with faith into the Universe. I feel an abundance of love around me. I am one with the Universe, I am supported by its angelic energy. I feel love within my being in every breath, with every step forward. I am flowing with the rivers of time, I am blessed.

Each day you will get a bit better than the last, and even if you don't feel like you are getting better, trust and believe that it is happening. But you still need to do the work to move through this energy. A Spiritual Awakening has opened a new door for you, and this door has elevated your consciousness, it has opened your mind in a way that it has never been before. Every thought and feeling you are experiencing right now is valid, and you need to accept it so that you can move through it.

Before we learn how your life is going to change, I want to remind you of a useful technique to come back to at any time during your Spiritual Awakening process. This technique will help ground your soul into your body, and call upon your Higher Self to come forth and appear. Grounding your soul, connecting with your intuition and living in the present moment are going to be your greatest tools to navigate this period of your life. You are processing a lot of information, your cells are changing and transforming as your vibration is raised to a new level to match your new frequency of heightened awareness.

Self-Soothing Technique

Place your hand on your heart and close your eyes. Press gently onto your chest so you can feel the weight of your hand on your skin and imagine feeling the nurturing love and supportive energy from your Higher Self coming through the spirit realm and into your body as you say the following sentences:

"I am not alone."
"You are here with me."
"I love myself."

Remember:
You are stronger than you realize.
You have more courage than you can imagine.
You are beautiful, talented, and worthy of miracles.
Everything in your life is perfectly timed and coming into alignment.

Repeat this technique as often as you like and call upon angels, spirit guides, or ancestors to help guide you through this feeling into a place of healing. To help navigate this awakening process it's important to take as much time as you need to nurture yourself. Like all difficult challenges in our life, we need to honor and be present with ourselves as we enter the darkness. Try to hold comfort in knowing that this phase will pass, that it will move through you, and that with time, profound wisdom will take its space.

Your Soul Craves Change

The beginning stage of your Spiritual Awakening process may feel quite isolating. The activities that once brought you joy hold no meaning anymore, and you may even prefer to spend your time in your own misery of depressive thoughts or anxious feelings. You might feel as though you have lost your identity of who you were, for now you are seeing your world around you in a completely different way. In a way that you don't understand. Your inner peace is being tested, your connection with your divine self is being brought out into the light. Nothing is making sense; you may feel abandoned, alone, and hopeless. The unknown that is laid out before you feels scary and almost impossible to navigate. You are holding firm to your beliefs, yet nothing in your life is telling you they are true; in fact, you realize that you have been living in an illusion and that illusion has been shattered. Your whole world is flipped upside down. Everything that you once knew doesn't make sense anymore and you wish that you could go back to how it used to be. How you once were. How you thought life should be—B.C—before consciousness. But the truth is that you now realize you had been living unconsciously, you had been living in a dreamlike state, perhaps one that involved following the ideas of others, or chasing fickle vibrations. But now you are waking up and realizing the truth; you need to unlearn everything that you thought you knew to relearn and remember the true meaning of your divine existence once more.

The concept of letting go of who you once were can feel exhausting! You are releasing not just this lifetime, but many lifetimes before of conditioning and inherited belief systems that are actually causing you more harm than good. The beginning stage of this realization may incur depressive thoughts or anxious feelings, so remembering how to self-soothe using the techniques we learned about earlier will help you. When entering the Spiritual Awakening process you need to do whatever you can to make yourself feel better. Resort back to your list of how to nurture love to your soul (page 73). It's very common to feel sadness, grief, and anger as you mourn your old way of life, the old you, and most likely you weren't ready to give that up. But something happened, something changed and pushed you onto this unknown pathway. So stay strong, because the new you, the version of you that you are stepping into is exactly who you have always wanted to be. You are becoming the very best version of yourself that you ever thought possible. What you are about to embark upon is going to be the most exciting change you have ever experienced in your entire life! Everything in your life is about to transform for the better. So, take a deep breath and know that you are not alone.

Some people experience a "Dark Night of the Soul" (this is a term that dates back centuries), as they enter their Spiritual Awakening process. The Dark Night of the Soul is the process of breaking through the illusions of our identity and ego.

Our ego seeks acceptance
but the Soul is complete on its own.

Our ego wants to be loved
but our soul is and has always been an abundance of love.

Our ego seeks validation
but the soul knows we hold eternal beauty within.

You may refer to yourself as the role that you play in this world—mother, father, sister, brother. Or your career and purpose—doctor, teacher, healer, lover—but these are all just labels, masking who we really are. The death of your ego is the end of who you think you are and a rebirth into who it is that you've always been—a divine light being of creation. The Dark Night of the Soul is the destruction of your beliefs and identity in this world. But remember, this identity is just a mask that you have decided to wear. Your true identity is wholeness. The real you is an abundance of divine pure energy of love who is connected to the Universe at all times. The ego focuses its attention onto an identity, whereas the truth is you are and have always been an angelic entity connected to the cosmos. Not all awakenings have a Dark Night of the Soul, but a large majority of them do. We can have a Spiritual Awakening while realizing that everything in our life is perfectly fine and happy, but still it doesn't make sense nor bring us true fulfillment, thus encouraging the questions of self-discovery to present themselves before us once more.

This first stage of healing is accepting your current situation and releasing the stagnant energy that is holding you back. Surrender all of your fears, worries, and stress into the Universe and allow the divine source of creation to transmute that energy into greatness, so that you may walk your path with confidence once more.

We journey through the Spiritual Awakening process as we would with any area of our life that needs healing. We locate the energy within our aura that needs healing, refer to the spiritual techniques that resonate with us and use them to assist the transformation to take place with gratitude. Our goal is to harmonize the energy of our mind, body, and soul once more. So, the first stage is to look carefully at the energy within your body and see where it is stuck, and focus solely on self-soothing and self-loving.

Ritual to Heal Whilst in a Spiritual Awakening

Intention:
This ritual is to support my healing process so that I may move through this Spiritual Awakening with wisdom and grace.

Sacred Space:
Fire Energy: I call upon the energy of Fire. May the warmth of your love transform the pain in my body so that I may journey through this Spiritual Awakening with ease.
Water Energy: I call upon the energy of Water. May your soft currents soothe my worries and fears as I navigate the unknown before me.
Earth Energy: I call upon the energy of Earth. May your nurturing care ground my soul as I enter boldly into this Spiritual Awakening with confidence.
Air Energy: I call upon the energy of Air. May your wisdom be heard loudly as I learn how to heal my wounded heart.

Action: Energy Healing

1) In a meditative state, close your eyes and ask to be shown where in your body you are holding on to energy that needs to be released.

2) Once you have identified the energy, as we explored on page 160, focus on clearing and cleansing this energy using any of the healing techniques we explored in the section "Nurturing Your Soul" (page 48). Or try the following:

3) Feel the weight of your body on the surface which you are sitting or lying down on. Sitting up is best for this exercise. After you

connect with the surface, allow yourself to become very heavy, sink deeper into relaxation. Envision roots from your pelvis connecting to the Earth and sinking deeply into the core, where the molten lava resides.

4) The fire of the molten lava has the ability to transform energy, so focus on this connection as you release and surrender any energy that is causing you pain. Feed that pain through the roots that you have grown into the core of the Earth. Scan through your body, slowly starting at the top of your head all the way down to your toes. Find any energy within that is holding you back from being your true self and let go. Use your breath to move this energy and push it down through your energy channel into the core of the Earth. Release this energy completely.

5) If you feel ready, choose an activity that will help nourish and replenish your energy. Find a technique that resonates with you the most; refer to "Recharging Your Energy" (page 72). Or use your visualization to imagine beautiful, nurturing vibrations flowing down upon you from the Universe into your crown chakra (the top of your head). Allow that energy to nurture love to your soul.

Once you have focused on cleansing and replenishing your energy, make a habit to do this often. Whenever you feel uneasy or hurt, know that this is a time that your energy is evolving. The molecules in your body are changing as they expand and reflect the changes that will be taking place in your new level of consciousness.

It's helpful to seek support from accredited healers as you will be entering a new territory that you are unfamiliar with. There are wonderful healers in the world, with many more feeling the calling to help people just like you going through this difficult emotional experience. Research some energy healers in your area; ask for recommendations from friends, or at a local yoga/ meditation studio or organic shop. See what feels right and try out a few variations. Allow yourself to be naturally drawn to a form of therapy and learn about it.

A Spiritual Awakening can bring forth a sense of hopelessness, so we want to take that power back. And how do we do that? We turn to journaling. We connect with our intuition to seek guidance. As you navigate your Spiritual Awakening, your intuition is going to be your strongest tool for survival.

Action: Journal

Always start your journal entry with today's date, and write down your story. Give your emotions the acknowledgement they deserve. If you feel like you need to cry and grieve this part of your life, give yourself permission to do so. When we express our story we accept it as part of our journey too, and release the energy. If we resist the energy from moving we will stay in pain. So express everything that you possibly can. Answer questions such as:

What happened to bring this Spiritual Awakening on?
How does it feel and what emotions have arisen?
What beliefs have been challenged?
Have any boundaries been crossed?

Once you have released your story, and have self-soothed, look to the following questions to gain more insight.

Is my soul requesting a change of path?
Do I need to listen to my intuition more?

Am I not practicing self-love, self-respect, or self-acceptance?

Is my soul tired?

Do I need to soothe my energy with nature?

Should I surround myself with more open-minded people?

Do I need to remove anyone in my life?

Do I need more love in my life?

Do I need to establish and communicate my boundaries?

Have I put myself in the wrong environments or scenarios?

What am I doing in my life that is harming my growth?

What am I not doing that could help my personal development?

What does my soul need?

Am I grounded right now?

Examples of things that you need to change could be seeing people who you know aren't good for you. Doing things that are not benefiting you in the long term. Feeding your body harmful food or substances. Or what are you not doing that you should be doing? Are you not getting out and exercising? Are you not giving yourself permission to grieve? Are you ignoring what is going on right now? The answer could be very varied across many channels. It could be that you are reading this book but aren't doing the journaling exercises! Journaling is how we allow our soul to speak, and right now, you soul has something to say to you.

After this, it's important for you to remind yourself that you will get through this. Even though we don't know what transformation is taking place, and we may not for awhile, we need to trust that this is meant to happen, it's happening for a reason, and the only way through this is to have complete faith in the divine power of the Universe.

Ritual Closing:

Give gratitude to the energies that you called upon. And make note of any specific insight that was achieved through the process. Recite your intention as though it has been done:

"I have healed the energy from my Spiritual Awakening."

"I am open to receiving the wisdom from my Spiritual Awakening."

"I am thankful for this profound wisdom and Spiritual Awakening."

Now that you have released the energy that was causing you pain, it's time to self-reflect over your life. We need to reveal the limiting beliefs that are holding you back from being true to yourself. We spent some time exploring this on page 193 in relation to your inner child, but in this next section, we'll go through your unconscious behavior, where some limiting beliefs may be stored. We want to bring forth everything into the light. Now is your chance to start fresh, so let's examine every area.

Shadow Work

The shadow self is a Jungian psychological term used to describe the dark side of our personality that we unconsciously disown or suppress. The shadow self holds qualities, emotions, and feelings that we know exist, but refuse to accept to be a part of ourselves and so we move them over to the side of our shadow where we can't see them. Most often the shadow consists of negative attributes such as rage, jealousy and shame, but with each negative comes positives too and so when we suppress one emotion we are also suppressing many others. As we journey to uncover the truth of our shadow we have the ability to clear outdated beliefs, tap into unconscious potential, and reveal our hidden desires.

Shadow work is the activity of confronting, acknowledging, and befriending these hidden attributes of ourselves through self-reflection and self-awareness. When we become aware of our shadow self we can live authentically, by accepting that both the light and dark of ourselves exist harmoniously together. Even though we choose to align ourselves with positivity and lightness of being, darkness exists within us, because both sides are needed to create wholeness. We must acknowledge these energies are a part of us too in order to be balanced and to have control over our life.

Let's look at the following example to further understand this: Someone has done something to you that causes you to feel an angry and irritated reaction. You believe that to feel angry or irritated is a trait that belongs to a "bad" person, and in fear of being perceived that way, you suppress and deny these emotions within you. But perhaps in this particular circumstance you had been suppressing feelings of anger for many years and at this time, your anger explodes, even though the situation didn't warrant such a powerful response. But because you had been bottling up these emotions for so long, your unconscious shadow overtook your consciousness, forcing you to act irrationally, extremely angry, and very "out of character." You need to befriend the shadow self and make the unconscious conscious so that when faced with a situation that causes you anger, you express that anger in a healthy and controlled way. When you suppress anger you are withholding other qualities as well, such as your opinion, your voice, and your passion. When we hold back on these elements of ourselves we are disowning our own humanity, and this can lead to an imbalance of our emotional wellbeing. Recognizing our anger is a form of self-reflection and being self-aware (two key attributes for personal development and growth). The emotion of anger is telling you that something has upset you; when it arises, pause and ask what it is here to show you. Learn from it and accept that this emotion exists and make peace with it as being a part of who you are.

Let's look at another example: Your friend has succeeded dramatically in their business. But instead of feeling true happiness for them you find yourself resenting them with bitter jealousy. As these feelings arise, instead of denying them, ask what are they are here to teach you. Maybe the feelings of resentment and jealousy are masking the motivation within you to attain the success that your friend has; therefore, you are suppressing both the feelings and the motivation (the positive attribute of that shadow self). Or perhaps the feeling of jealousy has arisen because hidden in your psyche you hold a limiting belief about your ability to achieve your own success. Perhaps when faced with this situation your shadow self took over your consciousness and refused to acknowledge nor celebrate and instead you ignored their calls and spoke badly about them behind their back. These actions aren't your usual manner; it was your shadow self acting out unconsciously. It was your shadow self who was doing it to protect you. Your ego created your shadow self as a form of protection. Maybe this protection relates to a memory in your childhood where you tried to succeed but failed and instead of learning that failure isn't bad and that it's a form of growth, you connected the two together and created a limiting belief that you are incapable of succeeding. And so, instead of confronting this limiting belief that is holding you back from being your true self and stepping into greatness, you react with jealousy and discredit another, thus ignoring your true desires and allowing this limiting belief to stay alive.

There's always a reason behind your feelings and the more you become conscious of them, accept them, and learn from them, the more authentically you will live and the greater wisdom you will attain. You always have the power within to discover what it is that makes you happy. You have the ability to change your reactions through changing your perception of your life. We are all on our own journey and we should never compare; it's okay to want success when you see someone else rise, but know that by supporting another and cheering them on doesn't lower your own possibility of succeeding. When we support another's success it brings our own vibration up higher too, thus bringing us closer to our own success and illuminating our desires, for we are becoming comfortable with those high vibrational feelings of happiness and celebration.

Suppressing any feelings or emotions can lead to physical stress of the body. We are trying so hard not to identify with these emotions, assuming that they are "bad," but to feel these emotions is to be human. Let's remind ourselves that we are a Spiritual Soul, experiencing our life on the human plane. These emotions are a part of our journey.

As we embark upon the pathway to reveal our shadow self we must first ensure we begin from a place of grounding. For as we confront these dark sides of us we need to face them with kindness and self-compassion. Shadow work is usually done with your journal in a safe space. Feel the support of the Earth beneath you, ensuring you feel stable, grounded, and secure. Remind yourself of the power you hold, that you are the creator of your life, and that by revealing your shadow self, you are enabling your consciousness to be whole, thus providing you with inner peace. When we learn how to accept and acknowledge these hidden parts of ourself, we have more control over our reactions and are able to view our world with a wise perception of our life.

Ritual for Shadow Work

Intention:
I accept both the light and dark within me. I know that the journey to wholeness is to honor both sides.

Sacred Space:
Fire Energy: I call upon the energy of Fire. Come forth to illuminate the truth of my darkness so that I may be at peace.
Water Energy: I call upon the energy of Water. Assist me in this ritual so that I can reveal the depth of my shadows and flow along the river of life once more.
Earth Energy: I call upon the energy of Earth. Let me surrender my fears into your womb of love so that I may walk my pathway with courage and confidence.
Air Energy: I call upon the energy of Air. Come forth with your soothing vibrations to lead the way for my shadow self to be revealed.

I call upon Grandfather Sun, Grandmother Moon, my ancestors and spirit guides. Come forth and support me as I confront and heal my shadow self.

Action: Journaling

Shadow work requires diligent self-reflection to bring forth self-awareness. When these two qualities are attained in our persona, we are capable of handling any situation with wisdom and grace. The more we self-reflect, the easier it becomes to analyze our reactions and thoughts, providing greater understanding for our own true desires and beliefs to reveal themselves.

Refer to the shadow work journaling exercises on the following pages and when you are ready close your ritual.

Closure:

Thank the Universal Energies for their presence, making specific reference to any wisdom that was learned. Signal the final closure of the ritual by saying an affirmation to support the knowledge learned. Something like, "I accept my shadow self," or be specific as to the emotions/ attributes that you revealed, "I accept ... aspect of myself."

Shadow Work Exercises:

Start your journal work by analyzing your judgements on other people and recall specific encounters that generate a strong reaction. List the people in your life that you may know or don't know who irritate you, whose presence annoys you, infuriates you, or angers you.

What qualities does ... hold that angers/ irritates/ makes me feel threatened or frightened?

What do they do specifically that causes me to have a strong reaction?

Then look within as to how these qualities that you dislike are within yourself too. Accept that they are a part of you and reveal the truth of their meaning.

What does this emotion/ reaction/ feeling have to teach me?

Is there a limiting belief attached to it?

What other attributes am I suppressing by bottling up this feeling?

Maybe there is someone who is bossy and their actions are annoying. Secretly, there could be a part of yourself that you wish would be more assertive, but instead you choose to ignore that true desire and be passive aggressive toward this bossy person based on your past experience, limiting beliefs, and general understanding that this archetype is more comfortable to you. But if you revealed the truth of why you feel the way that you do you could tap into the unconscious potential of being your own boss and role model.

Perhaps you are jealous of another person's ability to express their sexuality easily, either through their clothes or language and so you find yourself repulsed or angered at their liberty of being themselves explicitly. Sexual feelings and expression is within you too, but perhaps you have been raised to think that this side of yourself is evil to be shown, so you suppress it. But you don't realize that as you suppress your sexuality you are also suppressing your creativity and your freedom. This is why we need to be aware of our shadow self and the feelings and emotions that we are suppressing because 1) we are withholding more than just that emotion and 2) if ignored it can outburst in ways that we cannot control and usually don't intend. 3)

By bringing our darkness out into the light we are able to tap into unlimited potential (in this case, the ability to express ourselves creatively).

With each quality that you find yourself irritated, frightened, repulsed, or angered by, look to see where that attribute is within you too. Are you suppressing these qualities or do you wish to bring these qualities out but are unable to do so? Write in your journal or speak out loud in the mirror something like: "Even though I am ... I love and accept myself. I acknowledge that ... and I am working on myself to heal this limiting belief/ to harness this untouched potential."

For the next journaling exercise, choose someone close to your (your parents, siblings, or best friend), and pull out 5 - 10 traits within them that you don't like, or that resemble the negative parts of the shadow. Look at the list and see if any of those traits live in you. Where did they come from? Why do they exist? From here, look for the positives of their "negative" attributes to help find peace and understanding for another's actions. Refer to the example below to help explain this:

My partner is greedy with money. She/ he believes that by gaining more money they will feel more security at home, thus providing more happiness. On the positive, I don't stress about financial troubles because we always have enough. But on the negative, I am aware that the need for financial security is addictive and that money doesn't equal happiness. She/ he thinks this way because they grew up with little money. For this reason I am compassionate when approaching this subject and I make an extra effort to create our own sense of security and happiness at home through providing stability and love.

For every negative there is a positive to be gained and the more we explore the negatives within us and our loved ones, the easier it is to find the wisdom. In order to completely step into the positive, we must first own the darkness. We must acknowledge, accept, and make peace with this side of ourselves. Reminding ourselves that both light and dark is needed to create whole. Without dark, the light cannot shine. Both are needed in order for each other to exist.

Self-Reflecting and Self-Awareness Exercises

Recall a time in your life where the situation did not play out to your advantage. Perhaps the other person "won" or no one did. There was a disagreement of opinions and no solution made sense.

Write down what happened according to your point of view.

Why did this situation upset or anger me?
How did I react when things didn't go my way?
Why was my action, opinion, or decision right?
What outside influences impacted this decision?

Now write down what happened according to the opposite person's point of view.

Why did the situation upset or anger them?
Is there a reason why they behaved this way?
Why do they believe they were right?
Why did they dismiss my action, opinion, or decision?
Were they unable to see my point of view clearly?
How could I have relayed the information better?

Although no resolution needs to come forth as a result of this argument, what we need to understand and make peace with is a difference of opinions. If we can move our perception of the world to see another's viewpoint, it will help us bridge the gap between our differences of opinions. Sometimes there is no wrong or right way, and sometimes, the right way is completely logical and ethical. Helping others and yourself understand the right pathway can only be achieved through explanation, compassion, and understanding. We need to meet one another at the same level of consciousness to relay information properly. And be open to understanding that maybe we ourselves, are also at fault. Accepting and owning responsibility is an imperative act of growth. The more we recognize how we can do better, the greater the evolution of our soul can become.

Someone who holds characteristics that you disagree with is your personal opinion and perception. Neither your nor their opinion is right or wrong; it's just another layer of the "whole" spectrum. Help yourself see the world from their point of view by learning why they are the way that they are so you can hold compassion for their qualities that you don't agree with, instead of reacting with negative emotions. Our life path has the power to influence our personality and the more we learn about one another the easier it becomes to have compassion. We are all human, trying the best to live our life and are acting according to our own level of awareness.

Through self-reflection and self-awareness you are able to reveal the masks you have gathered to conceal the true you. It is the process of revealing you in your authentic self, which is the goal in our life. To become one with our soul, to live authentically, and to share our authenticity with the world.

Your Journey of Self-Discovery

Now that you've moved through the first stage, and spent as long as you needed completely engulfed in your confusion (and as you should; darkness is a wonderful lesson in itself), you will have now grounded yourself, accepted your life path, and fed nurturing love into your energy, enabling you to be present in this second stage as you develop a great thirst for knowledge for what your life could be. Questions that encouraged your journey of self-discovery such as "who am I?" "where am I going?" and "how did I get here?" will have surfaced. Although we may have determined the answers to these questions before out of curiosity, now we realize that we need a deeper meaning behind them, or perhaps the ideas we had formulated in our younger years do not reflect our mature attitude. And so, we commence our journey of inner work, connecting to our intuition and speaking to our Higher Self as we probe questions, learning the truth of what it is that we hope to achieve in this life. And as our priorities shift, our perception of the world around us changes too; the breaking through of our shattered illusion of reality is complete as we realize an entirely blank canvas is laid out before us. We have the ability to create the life we have always wanted.

In this stage of your Spiritual Awakening you will have a deep craving for purpose. Light conversations won't satisfy you anymore and you begin to examine every area of your life with scrutiny. Your soul is asking for a new environment to thrive in. Your soul has a clear idea of the person you wish to become and the life you need to live and in this stage you will move things around to reflect that internal need. As you explore your current situation, your job, your lifestyle, your friends, ask yourself the simple question of "does this serve my highest good?" "Does this support the life I want to lead?" And if it doesn't, become comfortable with letting it go and inviting in new vibrations.

You may find that you are surrounded with difficult situations that you cannot leave, and although the answer to remove these from your life is clear, you have a duty of commitment to family members, jobs, or limited funds to support your children, forcing your survival to take charge. Know that you can still find the peace that you seek amidst difficult circumstances, for you are changing your perception of the world. When your internal world changes, your external world reflects that change too. Stay strong in connecting with your intuition and find a way to support your need for change whilst honoring the survival needed for yourself and others.

Despite the circumstances you have been given in this life, you have the ability to change your destiny. Yes, our Soul Contract is written (the lessons we need to learn and the evolution of our soul's energy), but the environment in which you choose to learn those lessons can change. And you have the power to change your lifestyle, your friends, your work life. Almost every element of your life is possible to be changed to reflect the new you.

Right now in this moment you have the power within your fingertips to create the life you have always craved. The question is, what kind of life do you want? To find the answer to this we need to talk to our soul and learn what it is that our heart truly desires. The more we recognize the areas in our life that bring us joy and pleasure, the more we can decorate our world to be an environment that our soul can wholly thrive in. Finding the answers to these questions takes time and patience. It's important to note that the criteria for what brings you pleasure today will not translate throughout your entire journey in this world, for you are constantly evolving and changing; it is only natural that the desires of your heart evolve too. It will, however, be a natural progression from one to the next, but it is up to you to be aware and check in with yourself to learn these answers.

As you journal through the questions be raw, open, and truthful. Remember that the secret to living a fulfilled life is through being authentic and sharing that authenticity with the world, and so this next journaling exercise will bring forth this great revelation. We will ask questions that reveal who you wish to be, the life you want to lead, and the relationships you want around you. Be sure you have established a strong connection with your intuition as you journey through and ask these questions.

Journaling Questions to Manifest the Ultimate You

Imagine the best version of yourself possible.

What is a day in my life like?
What does it feel like to be me?
What are my relationships like with everyone around me?
What personality traits do I hold?
In my current life, what do I need to change to become the person I want to be?
Are there any relationships I need to remove?
Are there any lifestyle choices I need to stop?
Are there any parts of myself that do not believe that this version of myself and my life could happen?
What do I need to do more of to step into this version of myself?

Now examine your current life and see where in your life is not meeting up with your answers. What areas of your life do you need to change to reflect who it is that you wish to become? And when you identify the area of your life that needs to change, how are you going to change it? Write down your goals for this manifested version of the ultimate you and with each goal write down how you can achieve it.

Journaling Questions to Manifest Your Soulmate

If you are in a relationship, as you go through these questions and manifestations, check in with yourself and see how this matches back with your current partner. Perhaps there are some areas you wish to work on, and this is an opportunity to ignite a healthy conversation about your personal desires and needs for fulfillment.

If you are single, this is a great time to explore the kind of partner and relationship that you truly want. As you visualize this person, try not to have a particular someone in mind. Just imagine the feeling that they represent and the feeling that you are emitting.

What does my soulmate look like?
What does my soulmate feel like?
How do I feel when I am with them?
What kind of energy does my soulmate radiate?
What is our relationship like together?
How does my soulmate treat me?
What things do we like to do together?
What are the qualities and traits of my soulmate?
What's important to them?
Do we have the same priorities?

As you look over the traits of your true love, look at the things you would like to do together or what kind of qualities this person has. If you imagine your relationship bonding over travel, then get out and travel. Perhaps you want to enjoy spending time going for hikes together, so get involved in your local community hiking group. Getting out of your usual comfort zone is how you grow, develop confidence, and meet new people.

Journaling Questions to Manifest Your Dream Life

Imagine your dream life and then answer the following questions:

How do I spend my day?
What is the environment like that I live in?
Do I live in a busy city, a small country town, perhaps a laid-back beach lifestyle?
What is the kind of environment that I would thrive in?
What are the things that are important to me?
What kind of food do I nourish my body with?
How do I nurture my mind?
Am I in a state of peace?
What can I let go of in my current lifestyle to achieve this bliss?
What kind of improvements can I make in my current daily life to get to this place?

Once you have written the answers for your dream life, write down the answers for what your life is like now. Specifically for the questions "how do I spend my day" and "what is the environment like that I live in?" What elements in your life are reflecting your dream life and what areas of your life do you need to change? If you wish to feel confident and secure in your decisions in your daily life but you aren't feeling this way now, why aren't you? And what can you do to change this? If you are seeking confidence in your body and personality, start with internal work such as the self-love and self-care exercises (page 121). From here, nurture your body and mind to support the vibration you wish to embody. If you are lacking confidence over your career, how can you improve and support that? Find a local mentor, or study extra activities online. If you need confidence to speak with others, get involved with community groups and local classes. Encourage yourself to get out of your usual limits, and see the world that is around you. There is so much for you to explore, you just need to take the first step!

Journaling Questions to Manifest Your Career

How do I spend my work day?
Who are the people that I work with?
What is my ultimate dream job?
What makes me happy?
What am I good at?
What qualities come naturally to me?
What do I love doing?
What do I think is the most important thing that the world needs to heal from?

From these answers brainstorm some job ideas. Don't focus on whether you can get to this space; know that anything is possible and you need to dream big. From your answers write down a few career ideas (or just one); we will call them seeds. These are your seeds you wish to plant to bring the manifestation to life. But it's not just enough to plant the seed, you need to do the work, and allow the Universe to support you and open the doors for you to walk through. In your journal start a new page for each career idea/ seed and answer the following questions:

Career Idea (Seed)
What talents do I need to support this career?
What education do I need to support this career?
What experience do I need to support this career?
What talents, education, or experience do I already have of the list above in relation to this career?
How can I gain these missing talents, experience, and education?
What can I do today to support this seed coming into fruition?

When creating any goal you need to ensure they are specific, measurable, achievable, realistic, and time-based. Now that you have your goals written down before you, add to them, change them, rewrite them over and over again. This is your chance to co-create your destiny with the Universe! From each goal of what you want to manifest and invite into your life, ask yourself what you can do to help create that. How can you bring forth that idea into your life? We can't expect our career, or true love to come to us if we don't do anything to help generate it; we need to make an effort as well. What you give out you will receive in return.

Once you have clarity over your goals, follow through with the manifesting ritual to call this energy into your life.

Manifestation Ritual

Intention:
I am manifesting the life I want.
I am manifesting my true love.
I am manifesting to be ...

Sacred Space:
Fire Energy: I call upon the energy of Fire, the great creator of miracles. Come forth and transform this energy to enable my manifestations to come into fruition.
Water Energy: I call upon the energy of Water. The soothing vibrations of feminine fluidity. Come forth and wash over my fears that are holding me back from stepping into this reality that I choose to manifest.
Earth Energy: I call upon the energy of Earth. The nurturing love of Mother Nature. Come forth and keep me grounded as I navigate the unseen realms and harness the energy to manifest my greatest desires.
Air Energy: I call upon the energy of Air, pure lightness of being. Come forth and clear the pathway so that I may walk confidently and courageously toward my manifested dreams.

I call upon Grandfather Sun, Grandmother Moon, my ancestors, spirit guides, and angelic energies to help support my manifestations to come into fruition.

Action: Meditation
1. Get into a meditative state, feeling the support of the Earth beneath you. Ground your soul into your body and open up a channel of energy between yourself and the core of the Earth. Feel the nurturing love of Mother Nature supporting you.

2. Envision the galaxy of stars above you, and imagine a waterfall of silver stardust falling down upon you from the Universe above. This is manifested energy for you to create your dreams.

3. Allow yourself to feel the manifested energy from above in the galaxy and the love from Mother Nature below nurturing your soul. Let these two channels flow freely within your body.

4. Have a clear idea of what it is that you wish to manifest and imagine the energy that this manifestation brings. What does it look like? What would it feel like for this manifestation to be your reality? See it clearly before you. Speak your intention again and envision the energy of the silver rainfall from the Universe above to pour down over this manifested image.

5. While you allow the creation to take place, search within your body and see if there is any energy that does not believe that this manifestation will take place. Ask to be shown where in your aura you are holding yourself back from receiving this manifestation and then release that energy into the core of the Earth.

6. Repeat the steps above for at least 15 minutes, allowing yourself to completely embody the energy that this manifested goal could bring you. Focus on trying to raise your vibration to this higher frequency as you continue to release any energy into the Earth that is holding you back from believing it to be true.

Action: Creative Journaling
Depending on what you wish to manifest (love, lifestyle, career, or all three), write it out in a story form in third person. For example:

She/ he is brave, carefree, honest, and raw.

She/ he is living authentically in alignment with who they are by ...

She/ he lives in ...

She/ he spends their day ...

She/ he is in a loving and committed relationship with someone who is ...

Closure:

Give gratitude to the energies that you called upon, and any angelic beings that supported your ritual. Signal that the ritual is over by saying the words "and so it is."

The scientific reason behind visualization working is due to the chemical make-up of your brain. When you think about something, the neurons in your brain react the same way as if you were really experiencing it in real life. For this reason, what you think literally can become your reality. The more we emit pleasurable thoughts, the more we naturally navigate toward the opportunities that will bring forth more of this pleasure into our lives. This is why visualization and positive thought techniques work, because you are creating your energy at all times, and you have the power to make it positive or negative.

In order to achieve anything in this life we need to first define it; that means to write it down, speak it out loud, and establish what it is that you want. We call these our goals. And then, most importantly, we need to believe that we are capable of achieving them, that we are worthy of receiving these goals. Here, at this stage of belief, is when we can implement rituals and manifestations to support our goals. In our rituals we can harness these higher vibrations by shifting our energy frequency up toward our dreams and goals. During this stage of manifestation rituals we use the law of attraction principle of moving our body into a higher vibrational energy field to attract and connect to like-minded feelings, emotions, and vibrations.

Once we have visualized these goals through manifestations, we then also need to have an action plan to achieve these goals to bring the manifestation into fruition. It isn't just enough to want something or to manifest something. We need to be able to put a pattern together as to how this plan will come forth, how this manifestation will come into fruition. Setting intentions and manifesting desires are important to create so that the Universe knows what to send you. When manifesting we not only need to write it down, we need to imagine it, and we need to feel it.

When creating your manifestations they must be realistic and achievable. We must be flexible in our desires and allow the Universe to flow through the words and goals in effortless fusion.

Just because something doesn't happen, it doesn't mean that it won't; it means that something better is coming along in its place.

Stepping Into Your Power

The Spiritual Awakening process is uniquely different for everyone; the alteration to your awareness is created for your journey and yours alone. And although it may feel exhausting and devastatingly painful, hold comfort in knowing that this is part of your destiny, this great Spiritual Awakening is written into your Soul Contract. For when you finally do exit this stage of transformation, you will find yourself living your life with complete and utter bliss. You will find yourself having more honest conversations, deeper connections, greater confidence, more peace, more compassion, more understanding with yourself, your loved ones and this understanding will filter out into every area of your world. It's because of these positive outcomes that this experience is vital to the growth of your soul.

In the first stage of the Spiritual Awakening process you learned how to nurture your energy and accept your current situation. In the second phase we revealed who you really are, who you want to be, and what kind of life you want to lead. And now in the third stage you are able to create that life as you give yourself permission to step into your power completely by implementing changes to attain your goals. By this stage you know that the success and fulfillment of your life is all up to you! Instead of feeling dwarfed by this responsibility you arise to the challenge with enthusiasm for you know that this is a part of your Soul Contract. Before we adapt spiritual practices into our life, let's examine the importance of consistently creating healthy habits.

Opening yourself to rhythm and routine is how we find balance in our lives. And that same rhythm that we unconsciously turn to is what connects us to the Universal tides of life. Through routine we find ourselves with a sense of purpose, an understanding of self. And by showing the Universe your desired vibrations, you are setting your intentions with what it is that you wish to receive, purely by giving it first. And thus as the natural flow of Universal Energy goes, if you give what you seek, then it will be reflected in return.

The world is created in rhythms of routine. There is an ebb and flow, cause and reaction that enables the evolution of the world to evolve. Our bodies are designed with the same internal rhythm of the Universe, but often, we overindulge in outside influences and the wrong vibrations that are detrimental to our wellbeing thus interrupting our rhythm from flowing with ease. If we are able to strip back to the basics of who we are and what we need so that we may become aware of what is causing us harm, we will be able to make conscious changes that reflect our authentic self, and in return lead a long, fulfilled, and happy life.

The world is developing at a rapid rate and we are used to quick fixes; we want a pill to make us feel better instead of going within and doing the work ourselves. It's easier that way. But this is only a short-term fix. If we were to spend time knowing ourselves, loving ourselves, and nurturing ourselves, we would see a decrease in mental health, in disease, and also in crime. It would benefit the world as a whole. Right now the best thing you can do is lead by example.

Review over your journal work and explore what you have realized about yourself, about the life that you wish to live. What do you need to do to create the life that you want?

Analyze your daily routine and future goals. Strong emotions may surface as you explore the areas that command to be changed in your life. Let the voice of your intuition speak loudly, and trust your heart as you make the appropriate changes to your lifestyle.

When changing one of our habits that we have become extremely reliant on, we need to plan how and where that change is going to take place. The success of implementing positive changes and habits all comes down to planning. For example, perhaps you have been wanting to eat healthier but find it easier to resort back to what you know. You need to put some time aside each week to learn about why you need to eat healthier and how you can do it. In this time you may research healthy recipes to plan your weekly meals, and while doing so, learn the nutrients that each of those meals provide. Before going to the supermarket make a commitment to yourself and get in the habit of only filling up your fridge with heart-nurturing foods that reflect those recipes that you found. Lifestyle changes require education as well as implementation. We need to learn why we are making the change and how that change will be made before actually doing so; this way we are more likely to stick with the new habit.

Perhaps you have a difficulty letting go of negative thoughts and feelings, and you know deep down that consistent meditation would be so beneficial to you, but you can't seem to get into the habit of it. Choose somewhere in your day where you have time to apply this change, and choose something to do after it. Enforcing something after the change helps assist the memory of putting the action into place. Morning is a great time for meditation, so meditate and afterwards have breakfast. Or if you are too hungry, have breakfast, mediate and then clean your teeth. The cleaning teeth is your "after" to help cement the habit into place.

It also helps to visualize the process of adding a habit into your life to support this lifestyle change. Take a moment to imagine you changing your lifestyle to reflect your desired goals. Visualize yourself going through your day and doing it. Then imagine yourself in one month with that lifestyle change still in place but now you are seeing the results. If you were wanting to incorporate meditation daily perhaps now you see yourself as very calm, and completely content with your life. You're not trying to catch up or feel like you're chasing anything, you are just relaxed and ready for whatever comes your way. There is nothing that you can't accomplish! You are strong and successful in everything that you do. You will be more prepared to encounter life's challenges with deep inner peace in place, with an open and curious mind.

Daily Life Checklist

• Journal
• Meditate
• Make time for play
• Strengthen my intuition
• Pay attention to the signs
• Communicate with my soul
• Listen to the Energy around me
• Express my soul through creativity
• Connect with the Universal Energies
• Nurture my body with healthy foods and exercise

Your entire process of self-discovery is revealing the truth of what your soul needs. You have been listening to the voice of your intuition to lead you down this pathway and from doing so you have built strength and unshakable confidence to live the life that you have always wanted.

You will know that you have healed from your Spiritual Awakening (and that you have come out the other side), when you can look back at the trauma and be grateful for it. For without that specific situation, without that challenge, you would not see the world the way that you do today, and for that you are grateful. To get to this stage of acceptance and understanding takes time and patience. It won't happen automatically, there's no specific technique that will hurry it along; we have to do the work, we have to make the time. It will happen and you will be at peace when you learn how to lean in and embrace this new way of life. Once you have mourned the old you, and the old way of life, you can look toward the future with positivity and gratitude. And from here, your days will become filled with all the things that you and your soul truly loves, thus providing you with deeper fulfillment and greater rewards.

You now realize that because you have endured such a traumatic event and have come through the other side that you are truly strong enough to handle anything. With this knowing comes an immense sense of trust and safety in the Universe. You feel comfortable with the unknown, realizing that this is a part of the grand master plan of your Soul Contract. You don't have to worry about anything because you know that you are divinely looked after, and if you need answers, if you need security and safety, all you need to do is search within and ask your soul to show you the way forward.

Lean Curiously Into Challenges

Every challenge holds the potential to strengthen our connection with our soul. The more we learn how to lean into the voice of our Higher Self and to trust it, the better prepared we will be to handle any difficulties in our life. Why? Because the voice of our soul has complete clarity over the reasons why and how to navigate through this challenge for you to grow. The voice of our soul holds a clear perspective of our life path, and this information is available to us; all we need to do is move closer to love, let go of the fear, and listen to our soul.

In every challenge, ask yourself:
What does my soul need?
What does my soul want?

You have the strength to overcome any challenge that comes your way. There is nothing that you can't handle! But when faced with unfortunate circumstances, it's unlikely that we voluntary accept the pain and open ourselves to the lesson. Sometimes, when we are confronted with unexpected situations, we feel an internal trigger that pushes our mindset over to fear, or reveal a limiting belief that we think we can't control. We dismiss the wisdom of our intuition telling us that all is okay and instead we prefer to suffer in silence, screaming at the world for being unfair. But when we finally choose to step out of the victimizing cry to reflect over the situation from a different perspective, only then are we able to see the truth—that all change happens for a reason, and that reason is to support the evolution of your soul's energy, your own personal development to fulfill your Soul Contract.

When a job, relationship, or a friendship ends, this is a calling for a change of lifestyle. It's a calling to dive deep within ourselves and ask the questions:

Was I really the happiest I could be with that person?
Did that job really fulfill me?
Did my lifestyle support the best version of myself?
Could there be something better waiting for me around the corner?

Although the answers to these questions take time to formulate, what we know is that the current situation as it stands is provoking a deep insult to our soul. It needs attention and needs to be changed in order to realign with who it is that we are meant to be.

The Universe is always pushing you forward along the path of great victory, and it is only when we refuse to move that we find ourselves in deep pain. And too often, we focus for too long on the pain that we feel, rather than the great opportunity that is being presented to us. Remember, resistance = pain, acceptance = peace.

The next time you are faced with a challenge, check in with yourself and your own energy to see how you feel. Get into the habit of grounding yourself, realigning with your soul and listening to the voice of your intuition. Another grounding technique I love is a simple movement to bring your awareness to the center of your head, creating an immediate grounding and calming sensation. Try this exercise below:

1. Sit down on a chair and get into a comfortable position.

2. Find a spot on the wall that is your eye level to look at.

3. Continue to breathe gently as you gaze gently at this spot on the wall.

4. Move your awareness from being outside of you to being within you. Find the place just behind your eyes. Essentially move your energy and awareness back into your head. Feel yourself withdraw back into your body.

5. Allow your body to become very heavy as you continue to gaze straight ahead but from this new space of within your head.

Find the uncomfortable feeling within . . .
Sit with it.
Inhale and exhale.
Ask, "What is it here to teach me?"
Listen to the guidance.
Let it go.
Allow something new to be birthed in its place.

Facing challenges is difficult but it does get easier, because with each challenge you overcome your perception changes and your reactions become more neutralized. You learn to align with love instead of fear, and embrace and trust that there is a greater message to be revealed. You know that everything in your life is placed there for a reason. Remembering this can be difficult regardless of how much experience we gather, but the more you practice connecting with your soul, listening to your soul, honoring and nurturing your soul, the easier life will become. In this moment you can truly surrender everything that is holding you back from believing in yourself and step into alignment with your soul, enabling you to move through the difficult scenario to find the growth that you seek.

An invitation for transformation is laid out before me.
I'm standing in the waves of uncertainty
choosing which side I wish to fall.
Do I move toward fear or love?

If I choose fear, I will suffer
and allow myself to drown amidst my emotions.
I will be swamped in a whirl wind, a chaotic cloud of darkness.
A cloud that I have created for myself.

And if I choose love,
that means that everything I've ever believed in grows stronger.
I am supported by the Universe.
I am a creator of my dreams.
I am the architect of my future.

The answer is so simple, so why do I hesitate?
I check in with myself and I find…
I am ungrounded and I feel inferior of my power.
I am scared of the miracles that I am capable of.
I work through the limiting beliefs and I align with my soul once more to see
that there is nothing to fear for I am resilient and brave.
I have all the answers within me to navigate the life path I desire.
I just need to trust and believe.
I just need to let go to receive.

Align With Soul

You wake up empowered,
excited to see what the day will bring.
Your past is behind you,
you have healed and let go.
Your strength is now soaring
and you breathe with ease.
Knowing how perfectly timed your life is,
how beautiful the world has always been.
You feel love flowing from within your heart,
courage within your mind,
and peace inside your soul.
You are at one with the Universe.

Who Am I?

I am a divine light of angelic energy. I encompass both the masculine and feminine and I focus my attention on harmonizing the balance of these two energies within. Sometimes I lean more to one side than the other, and that's okay. That is what it is to be human and so I accept myself.

Who am I?

I come from a long line of lightworkers, whose ancestral energy lives on through me. I hold forth their dreams as their ideas weave effortlessly through my own. Enabling my own vision to breathe greater and wider. I feel their strength moving through me with every step forward.

Who am I?

I am traveling through this world as a piece of cosmic stardust, dancing through life, experiencing time as a human yet I am still my angelic self moving gracefully between the worlds of the seen and unseen.
I gather the wisdom needed from above, and harness the power from below and walk alongside this journey with you.
Thank you for walking with me.

How to Align With Soul

Congratulations! You've made it to the end of this book! Before you read the final chapter, let's reflect over the spiritual beliefs, tools, techniques, and rituals that have been shared.

In "Understand thy Soul" we explored what our soul is, what the Universe means, and what our reality holds. We learned about spiritual philosophy, our Soul Contract and life purpose. We learned that everything is energy, and that if we learn how to master harnessing this energy that we will lead a deeply rewarding and fulfilling life (page 15).

In "Nurture thy Soul" we learned how to soothe our own energy to enable a fulfilling life. We understand that we are an extension of the Universe and when we think of ourselves and our life in this way we learn how to utilize the abundance of natural resources around us to provide us with great healing and wisdom. We now know that we are never short of knowledge when we ask the energy of the Universe for answers and advice (page 48).

In "Listen to thy Soul" we examined the key fundamentals of spiritual living, and how strengthening our intuition to connect with our Higher Self plays an important role in the happiness and fulfillment in our life. We explored meditation and journaling, along with some alternative viewpoints to heal our emotional wellbeing and mental health by focusing on cleansing and replenishing the energy of our soul (page 76).

In "Honor thy Soul" we explored spiritual practices and techniques to incorporate into our daily routine to harmonize the flow of Universal

Energy through our mind, body, and soul. We practiced positive self-talk to encourage self-esteem and confidence, while learning the importance of communicating our boundaries to set the level of love and respect that we deserve (page 108).

In "Heal thy Soul" we focused on how to heal the common challenges that we are faced with in today's world. Providing a spiritual outlook to our problems with practical how-to techniques and advice, we are able to change our perception of the world, thus inviting in deeper peace and greater awareness for love and fulfillment (page 150).

In "Awaken thy Soul" we explored what it meant to transition through a Spiritual Awakening. We learned how to move through this great transformation with grace and courage by incorporating soul-searching questions and manifestation rituals that encouraged the voice of our soul to speak through as we journeyed deep within to reveal the truth of our existence (page 232).

If you remember to bring all of these spiritual tools and techniques into your life you will be able to align with your soul easily. You will be able to live the life you have always wanted to, simply by inviting that power back into yourself and allowing your Higher Self to guide you to provide you with the answers within. In this last section we will explore what it is to be authentically you. This is your truth, your divinity, to get out there and start living!

We have lightly touched on many subjects throughout this book. If any particular modalities have called out to you don't ignore that voice from within. Research about it, take a course from an expert leader, or have a healing session with a fellow lightworker. The more you go out and start doing, living and learning, the more clarity you will gain over your life and your soul purpose.

Living Authentically

Our journey of self-discovery is a life-long process. You are always going to be faced with challenges that test your connection with your Higher Self which have the power to push you further away or bring you deeper into its love. The side you choose to align with is up to you. We've learned that the more we lean into challenges the greater rewards we will receive and the closer we will feel to the divine love of the Universe. Having ultimate trust in its wisdom will bring forth the most rewarding life experiences, and holding a light-hearted view of our journey will create the love and peace that we seek. We are able to move into our position of power and authenticity simply by living life as ourselves.

The more consistent you are with living authentically, the louder your soul will speak. The more aligned you will live with your Higher Self, the more pleasurable your life will become. In order to live authentically, we need to be clear on who we are, and what we want. And the only way to reveal this truth is by taking the time to get to know our true self. Put time aside every day to reveal your divine authenticity by meditating, journaling, setting goals, planning, and creating actions on how to follow through to create the life that you desire. These simple concepts have the power to create a fulfilling and rewarding life, for not only are we allowing our intuition to guide us toward what it is that our soul craves, but the more we experiment and try things out the more positive reinforcements we will receive as our goals become clearer and attainable.

When you align with your soul you have built an unbreakable communication channel allowing the light of your intuition to guide you on your pathway. You have complete trust and faith in the

Universe, as you listen to the passions of your soul and live the life that you love. To live authentically is the goal of our life purpose, because from this place we know ourselves so well that we can move through any challenges with ease, opening ourselves up with wisdom and compassion to navigate the unknown waters before us.

We live authentically when we:
1) Communicate strong boundaries
2) Strengthen our intuition regularly
3) Listen and act from a place of love
4) Protect, cleanse, and nurture our energy
5) Create a healthy environment to thrive in
6) Practice self-compassion and self-discipline
7) Nurture our body with plant-based food and exercise
8) Love ourselves and accept ourselves exactly as we are
9) Create positive habits that nurture and honor our soul
10) Self-reflect often and hold self-awareness of our actions
11) Be flexible to change and have a curious approach to life
12) Harmonize the flow of energy between our mind, body, and soul

We have explored all of these ideas throughout this book, and many more to help support your transformation process. We've become more receptive of challenges realizing that they are the gateway to transformation which is the true essence of our Soul Contract. We have learned that in order to heal we need to accept and acknowledge our situation. We need to truly feel the emotions and energy that arise within us so that we can release and let go. The more aware we become of our own energy field and that of others the more it will enable a smooth transition into the pathway of our greatest selves. For we know that we are made of energy, and thus if we can master releasing and harnessing energy we will be able to create the life that we want with ease.

When we focus our attention on learning what it is that our soul wants, we then have a clearer understanding over the motivations for our decisions and are able to make choices with confidence. If we find ourselves hesitating we know to take some time to reconnect with our soul and ground ourselves. In this space we remind ourselves that we are always supported by our Higher Self and therefore, there is no wrong choice. As long as we are moving our lifestyle toward the life that we want, and we make sure that every action, word, and situation reflects our true desires, we are always going to find what we need to create the life that we crave. When we live authentically we have clarity over our priorities, and ensure that our needs are met first, because we know that from this place we can help others more easily.

When we live authentically we are able to let go of any energy or problems that do not belong to us with ease. We learn how not to attach ourselves to others' lives and understand that we are all responsible for our own power. We can lead the way to remind another of their own path, but we cannot walk the path for them. We can only remind them of the power that they have within.

When we live authentically we have no difficulty owning up to our mistakes, for we understand that mistakes hold an invitation of self-discovery and here is where we find the power to transform our perception of the world. We speak our boundaries boldly and unapologetically, knowing that when we give love to ourself first, we pave the pathway for the love and respect that we deserve.

When we live authentically we have strong spiritual practices in place, and we are comfortable journeying to the unseen realms and harnessing the abundance of energy that is around us. We know that the stronger our connection with ourselves becomes, the deeper our soul's growth of personal development will evolve.

When we live authentically we don't self-sabotage. Because we know that we are worthy of love. We spend time honoring and praising our soul, learning about ourself as manifested consciousness in this reality. We know that we are destined to create incredible things; how do we know this? Because you exist! You are living this life right now, you are reading these words. You are feeling the very beating of your beautiful heart moving through this space. You are feeling the energy of your soul.

No one sees the world the same way that you do. Your perspective, how you speak, the words you use, and the way you share your vision is completely unique and absolutely exquisite. You are beautiful and magnificent, and the world needs you in it. We need your gift, we need your healing energy and positive vibrations. You are a divine creation of the Universe, destined to create incredible things. Don't ever forget it!

Our inner journey is never complete because there is no final destination for evolution. We are constantly faced with challenges that encourage us to reveal a deeper layer of truth within us. Each phase of understanding raises our consciousness into a new vibration bringing forth peace, acceptance, and understanding. Thus aligning our Spiritual Self with our Higher Self, enabling the truth of our life purpose, the calling of our soul's wishes, to come forth. And the desire of our soul has one aim in mind—to live a life with deep meaning, full of experiences as we play out the depth of our destiny amidst the blank canvas of our wildest dreams. And together, we bring the magic of the unseen worlds right here into our awareness, weaving the dream for all to dance, sharing our love together as one.

My Journey to Authenticity

It took me a long time to recognize the truth of my life path. I had visions as a child, but I assumed they were a part of my wild imagination. And in return, I had been suppressing it, disowning it, doubting it, but from writing this book the truth has become very clear. As I journeyed to the unseen realms to gather spiritual wisdom to share, I learned about the truth of my past. That is, I come from a long line of witches. The energy from my ancestral line and my own past lives is vibrating brightly within my being. But I have taken a long time to truly harness this energy with loving confidence, even though the knowledge and wisdom has always been present. There was something holding me back from stepping into my power completely. As I journeyed deep within my own history, I understood very clearly as the fear of who I was still shone brightly. A memory of the witches who were killed for being their authentic self had scarred my heart; I was terrified to speak my truth. I had to remind myself that I am living in a different time. I am allowed to be who I am in this world. I am allowed to speak my thoughts clearly without being shamed nor burned. And it is with a clear voice and shaking hands that I say loudly and unapologetically, I am, and have always been, a spiritual witch.

In my next book, A Spiritual Witch, *I will share with you my story.*

Moving through the different frequencies of life's challenges,
I enter boldly.
There is no fear, no space within me to move over to a vibration
that is anything less than beautiful.
For it is love that breathes light within me
and it is love that I feel around me.
I walk through life knowing
that I have the power within me to heal myself.
I walk through life knowing that I have all the answers I need right now.
And I dance through my days with admiration
for such a spectacular world of mystic,
aligning with peace and patience for my life to unfold.
I do not rush, I do not worry.
For I know that I'm divinely guided by the Universe at all times.

about the author

Phoebe Garnsworthy

Phoebe Garnsworthy is an Australian female author who seeks to discover magic in everyday life.

She travels between the worlds of the seen and unseen, gathering ancient wisdom and angelic energy. Her writings reflect a dance with the mystical and wonderful, an intoxicating love potion to devour in a world that overflows with forgotten love and enchantment.

The intention of her writing is to encourage conscious living and unconditional love.

www.PhoebeGarnsworthy.com

Other Books by Phoebe Garnsworthy

Daily Rituals:
Would you like to attract more abundance? More love, more happiness and more peace? It is available to you right now, if you believe it to be true. Everything in existence is vibrating energy. Whatever you want can be yours – if you learn how to emit that vibrational frequency. And from this place, energy will magnetize toward you, naturally connecting like vibrations together. This enables you to attract what it is you wish to seek.

Sacred Space Rituals:
The pages of this book have been carefully created by calling upon ancient spiritual philosophy from around the world. They primarily use the principals of creative visualization while harnessing the abundance of Universal energies that surrounds you. The purpose of these rituals is to assist you in your journey of personal development and spiritual transformation.

Define Me Divine Me: A Poetic Display of Affection
Define Me Divine Me is an exploration of raw truth that provokes our deepest emotions so that we may honor both the light and the dark within us all. Together, we allow the words of enlightened wisdom and painful beginnings to wash through us, as we stand back up and claim what is rightfully ours.

and still, the Lotus Flower Blooms:
This spiritual poetry book explores the hardships we face throughout our life and inspires you to search within to find the tools you need to survive. Like the lotus flower who grows through mud yet rises everyday to greet the sunshine without a slither of darkness upon its petals, you will too, move through your life with grace, resilience and beauty. And still, the Lotus Flower Blooms.

Lost Nowhere + Lost Now Here

The **Lost Nowhere Series** explores spiritual Witchcraft in a fictional environment. While following the eclectic imagination of a young girl called Lily, the reader is taken to another Universe to a magical world called Sa Neo. In this enchanted world you will find seven lands, each representing our seven energy chakras. And those seven lands are filled with powerful Witches, Shamans, queens, kings and mermaids. The emotions and traits of each chakra is represented through the interesting village people and their actions. This fantasy world reflects Phoebe's true eclectic imagination as you witness a world of beauty, miracles and magic in vivid detail while learn spiritual wisdom on how to love yourself and your life in this fantastic series of fictional witchcraft.

A note from the author about the Lost Nowhere series:

The first books I ever read were fairytales, and as I grew up, I didn't want, nor did I believe, that fairytales needed to stop being read. I discovered magical realism novels as a young adult, and from here, my love for books only grew stronger. It was no surprise that the first book I ever wrote reflected my own desires. Although, with my new adult perspective, my books needed to contain depth and wisdom in order to satisfy my cravings. Incorporating witchcraft into fiction was a natural process for me as my entire childhood consisted of creating initiations and magic, (little did I know that I was tapping into wisdom from my past lives)! Writing the Lost Nowhere Witchcraft series was an absolute pleasure. I could see the enchanted world of Sa Neo so clearly in my mind. And as I journey through it, I take you with me, as we gather the wisdom of the world, the magic of its people, along with a new understanding of life, our reality and why we are here.

CPSIA information can be obtained
at www.ICGtesting.com
Printed in the USA
BVHW050246011221
622872BV00002BA/140